The Romance of Protestantism

The Romance of Protestantism

Tales of Trials and Victory

by

Deborah Alcock
author of *The Spanish Brothers*

INHERITANCE PUBLICATIONS
NEERLANDIA, ALBERTA, CANADA
PELLA, IOWA, U.S.A.

Canadian Cataloguing in Publication Data

Alcock, Deborah, 1835-1913.
  The romance of protestantism

  ISBN 0-921100-88-4

  1. Protestantism. I. Title.
  BX4815.A42 1999   280'.4   C99-910559-0

Library of Congress Cataloging-in-Publication Data

Alcock, Deborah, 1835-1913.
  The romance of Protestantism : tales of trials and victory / by
Deborah Alcock.
        p. cm.

  ISBN 0-921100-88-4 (pbk.)

  1. Protestantism—History. I. Title
BX4805.2A53 1999
280'4'09—dc21

                                               99-035037
                                                    CIP
                                                     AC

Cover painting: J.H. Isings *Luther at the Diet of Worms, 1521*
Used with permission from
Wolters Noordhoff b.v., Groningen, The Netherlands

All rights reserved © 1999 by Inheritance Publications
Box 154, Neerlandia, Alberta Canada T0G 1R0
Tel. & Fax (780) 674 3949
Web site: http://www.telusplanet.net/public/inhpubl/webip/ip.htm
E-Mail inhpubl@telusplanet.net

Published simultaneously in the United Kingdom by
Inheritance Publications (U.K.) 19 Tench Way, Romsey, Hants, SO51 7RX

Published simultaneously in U.S.A. by Inheritance Publications
Box 366, Pella, Iowa 50219

Available in Australia from Inheritance Publications
Box 1122, Kelmscott, W.A. 6111 Tel. & Fax (089) 390 4940

Printed in Canada

Contents

From *Doctor Adrian: A Story of Old Holland*
by Deborah Alcock, Author of *Crushed Yet Conquering*

PREFACE

"History never releases her slaves. He who has once drunk of that sharp, strong wine goes on drinking it, even to the end." So spoke Michelet, himself one of the priests of History. For History has her priests, who minister in her temples and convey her messages to the world. She also has her slaves, who do her humbler work — "temple-sweepers," as Ephesus was of old to the great goddess Diana. They do it willingly — yes, and very often they do it because they cannot help it. An impulse they cannot resist drives them on.

The following pages contain the substance of a few informal "Talks" actually given under such an impulse to a little company of friends, by one of these humble slaves of History, sold into her service in childhood, and kept at work chiefly in one particular corner of her vast temple. From this experience there has sprung up an ardent love for that especial corner, and an eager desire to reveal to others the treasures that are to be found there. Truly,

The passion of long years I pour
Into these words.

These Talks are in no sense a history of Protestantism — a theme infinitely too vast and complex to be treated thus. As well might the discoverer of a mine of diamonds, anxious to reveal his discovery and put it to use, think of carrying the mine about with him for exhibition. No; he would take with him a few of the stones he had found there, and show them as specimens. If he wished to be believed — anywhere outside of a lunatic asylum — he would not pretend that *all* the stones in the mine were diamonds, or even that diamonds lay about it in heaps, to be picked up without labour or trouble. That is not Nature's way. Nor will anyone conceive that the history of a mighty and complex movement, extending over more than a thousand years and involving many millions of fallible men, could be "all compact" of romance — of thrilling and dramatic episodes, or of deeds of supreme heroism, self-devotion, and magnanimity. That is not Nature's way in the moral any more than in the physical world.

Yet there are questions that would be asked, and rightly asked, of the "prospector" who brought the diamonds. "Are these diamonds genuine? And did they really come from the place where you profess to have found them?" These are questions of fact; and facts have to be substantiated by reliable testimony. If the prospector is wise he will have armed himself with such testimony, and be ready to produce it. We, too, have abundant testimonies to the genuineness of what we show and the truth of what we say. We Protestants appeal to history, and earnestly desire its investigation by every able, candid, and unprejudiced student.

Yet one more question would be asked of the prospector — "Granted that these are true diamonds, and that they come from that mine of yours, you have yet to prove that they are to be found there in number and in value sufficient to repay us for the toil and expense of working it; still more to enrich us all, as you so confidently promise."

This is really the crucial question — a question of proportion. The prospector's answer we do not know — our own answer we do know, full well. It is a glad and proud one: "There are plenty more where these came from." Amidst so much that one longed to tell — so much that burned in the heart and trembled on the lip — the difficulty has been only what to choose. Spain, with the grand and solemn tragedy of her *autos-da-fé*; Italy, the Niobe of nations, with her many noble sons slain in this cause to weep over; Austria, Hungary, Poland, and the Northern nations — all these have been left out — England but faintly touched upon, and Scotland scarce at all. And France? Between the death by fire of the first martyrs of the Reformation there in 1525 and of the last on the gallows in 1762, what sad yet magnificent stories have been left untold! What abysses of horror and anguish, what heights of triumphant faith and patience have been passed over! But we forbear. For, "Still they come, and still the cry is 'More!' "

Yet perhaps these very little Talks on a very great subject may induce some to search farther, and to explore for themselves the treasures of this mine.

There is one vast gallery which, properly speaking, is a part of it, but which yet does not fall within our province to enter. Protestant Missions, which in our own age have attained to such an immense development, have already a voluminous history, abounding in the elements of romance. But all this must be left to other hands. Our work is only with the days of our fathers, and with "the old times before them."

Two things, which yet would have greatly strengthened our case, will be found wholly absent from our Talks. We have, deliberately and of set purpose, left untouched the horrible details of cruelty — often of ingenious, diabolical cruelty — that meet us continually in the records of persecution and of martyrdom. There are things which, once read or heard, can never be forgotten again. They will not leave us; they haunt our memories; they come back to us when we desire them least, in our hours of gloom and depression, or, "In the dead unhappy night, when the rain is on the roof."

There are things which the eye can rest on — *must* rest on sometimes, if we are to read history at all — but the ear cannot bear to hear or the lip to utter them. The only comfort is, that they are past; and that, if those who suffered them could speak to us *now*, each one of them would say, "For me, I have forgot it all."

There is another case in which "silence is golden," though silence may mean the sacrifice of cogent and convincing arguments. We are silent about the worst and most terrible corruptions of the church that persecuted — often of the very persecutors themselves. We choose rather to think and talk of "whatsoever things are true, whatsoever things are honourable, whatsoever things are just, whatsoever things are pure, whatsoever things are lovely, whatsoever things are of good report." If we think of these things we shall find them — and nowhere more conspicuously than in the age-long struggle between the Faith of Christ and the errors and corruptions of Rome.

Editor's Note: The first edition of this book was published in October, 1908. The present edition is based on the second edition of March, 1909, and includes some minor editorial changes. The reader should remember that statements such as "four hundred years ago" means now about five hundred years ago.

WHAT IS ROMANCE, AND WHERE SHALL WE FIND IT?

All high deeds that make the heart to quiver
With a deep emotion as we read
Are Divine, and go back to the Giver;
Courage, high endurance, generous deed
Come from Christ, and unto Christ returning
Find their full acceptance only there,
In that Centre of all noble yearning,
In that Type of all perfection fair.
                              — MRS. ALEXANDER

REFORMERS OF THE SIXTEENTH CENTURY.

THE FRIARS' INTERVIEW WITH WYCLIFFE IN HIS SICK CHAMBER.

Reduced from "The History of Protestantism," by Rev. J. A. Wylie, by permission of Messrs. Cassell, Petter, Galpin & Co.

From *Hubert Ellerdale: A Tale of the Days of Wycliffe*
by W. Oak Rhind

I

WHAT IS ROMANCE, AND WHERE SHALL WE FIND IT?

Were it not well that we, who feel ourselves called upon to maintain the Protestant cause, should have some real acquaintance both with the history and also with the meaning of Protestantism? So shall we pursue our great conflict, not only because we think it useful, and necessary, and according to the will of God, but because we feel the glory, the beauty, the magnificence of that for which we have to contend — because we remember the mighty things that have been done by those who fought this battle in the old times before us, and the great cloud of witnesses with whom we are encompassed about. So great is that cloud that it tempts us to think, if the inspired author of the letter to the Hebrews had had to write his grand eleventh chapter in the Twentieth century instead of the First, what a Story he could have told! Well might he have said that "time would fail" him! We do not think his task would be finished yet — no, that it would ever be finished.

It is some broken fragments of that story which, as specimens of the whole, we would like to present to your notice when we ask you to think of the Romance of Protestantism — what does it mean, and what is it like?

But we must first ask another question — What is romance? I suppose the general idea of romance would be — stirring adventures, hair-breadth escapes, great deeds wrought, great perils faced, exciting stories. But these are not all. There might be all these, and yet no real romance. It would be a very exciting thing if a burglar were to leap from a high-up window with a lady's jewels under his arm — but would we call that romantic? I don't think so. We might call it romantic, however, if the house was on fire, and someone who knew there was a child asleep in the top storey, rushed in, saved the child, and leaped from the window with it in his arms. Especially if, though he did not know it at the time the child proved to be a near relation of his own — his brother's or his sister's child — that would indeed be romance.

What makes the difference? The high moral qualities engaged. The exciting adventures and all the rest are but the outward adornments — *these* are the things by which God touches our hearts, and shows us that the men and women who did them were inspired by that "breath of life" which He breathed into us at our creation.

Take, then, our motto as the definition of romance — "All high deeds that make the heart to quiver" — and they *do* quiver when we hear or read of them! But what are they? "Courage, high endurance, generous deed." And we must add something else. There would not be much romance in the world if we all stood separate, like grains of sand — near, yet apart from each other in mind and heart. No, it is the strong and tender human affections which make the most attractive part of all romantic stories. It may be the kind of love usually called romantic; or, just as truly, the deep, deep, love of friend for friend, of brother for brother, of parent for child, or of child for parent — and I will add another which has many illustrations in the theme before us — the love of the pastor for the flock and of the flock for the pastor. All these help to make true romance, and they will be found abundantly in the annals of that great conflict which, I believe, when all is told, will prove to be the grandest epic this world has ever known — the conflict of Faith and freedom with the superstition and the tyranny of Rome.

Nothing helps so much as illustration. Let us then take these four qualities of romance — courage, high endurance, generous deed, and strong and tender affection — and see if we can find them exemplified in the annals of Protestantism. Yes, the examples are so numerous — or rather so numberless — that it would take, not one hour's talk, but many, to exhaust them. And then they would not be exhausted after all.

Still, one fact or one story impresses the mind more than any amount of general statements. Take the first quality we have named — *Courage*. Where so many have stood the supreme test of courage by laying down their lives, how shall we choose? Just listen to a few words from the great historian Motley about the Protestant martyrs of one short period and one small country in Europe — "The chronicles contain the lists of these obscure martyrs, but their names, hardly pronounced in their lifetime, sound barbarously in our ears, and will never ring through the trumpet of Fame. Yet they were men who dared and suffered as much as men can dare and suffer, and for the noblest cause which can inspire humanity. Fanatics they were not, if fanaticism consists in show without corresponding substance. To them all was terrible reality. The Emperor and his edicts were realities; and the heroism with which men took each other's hands and walked into the flames, and women sang a song of triumph while the grave-digger was shoveling the earth upon their living faces was a reality also."

There were so many who died thus! But as the story of one man, which we can feel and realize means more to us than the bare mention of many, we will tell of Robert Glover, one of our own Marian martyrs. Others, in those days of trial, had gone to the stake with a smile on their lips and a deep joy filling their hearts, knowing that Christ was with them, and that they would go straight from the fire to see His Face. Not so Robert Glover. Deep despondency had laid hold upon him;

15

he thought that Christ had turned His Face away, and that, though he cried to Him in agony, the Lord had shut out his prayer. No voice, no answer came to him. All was dark. Yet still, with firm step and unfaltering heart, he went forth in the dark to die for Him.

There was with him a sympathizing friend — Austen Bernher, a Swiss, and formerly a servant of Latimer's, who had earned the honourable title of "The friend of the martyrs," for he gave himself to the work of comforting, encouraging, and sustaining them. He walked beside Robert Glover — the martyr with the firm step and the set, hopeless face. They came in sight of the stake. Then, suddenly, the face was transfigured, and a glad cry broke from the lips — "Austen, He is come! He is come!" Christ *had* come to him, in that strange, mysterious way which no man knows save he who receives the wonder and the joy. Not in joy only, but in rapture, the few remaining steps were trod. The fire was kindled, and in one minute and a half after it rose around him, he saw the Face of Christ.

It was as if he died, not so much by the anguish of the fire, as, "Heart-broke by new joy too sudden and too sweet."

I think that man's courage was supreme.

High endurance is another thing we expect to hear of in romance. For an example of that I will not ask you to look at the rack or the stake — only at a quiet room where a pale woman sits sewing. I do not think she is weeping: I think her tears will come later. What is she sewing? Only a shirt, "Seam and gusset and band, band and gusset and seam."

Ah! But this shirt she is making is for a singular purpose. She makes it by her husband's request. He lies in prison awaiting death for Christ's sake; and now the sentence has come, and the day is named. In the terrible days of the Marian persecution there came into use what has been called "The uniform of the martyrs" — the long, white shirt down to the feet which many of them wore at the stake; and Lawrence

Saunders had written to his true wife — "My wife, I would that thou wouldst send me that shirt whereof thou knowest the destination." And she did it! That was high endurance indeed. Think with what feelings she worked at her task, knowing — knowing all the time "its destination," yet "content," like the wife of another martyr, John Frith, to whom Tyndale wrote, "Your wife is quite content with the will of God." I think the endurance of these women was even greater than that of the men who faced the fire.

We ask now what *generous deeds* we have got to show. Take one for a sample, from the story of the Netherlands. Under the crushing tyranny of Alva hosts of martyrs and other innocent victims were slaughtered, until at last the people rose in the cities, the towns, and the country to shake off the intolerable yoke. It was not to be wondered at that those who were most active in the persecution should run some risk of having done to them what they had done to others.

The Burgomaster of Gouda had been particularly zealous in hunting the "heretics" to death. The people sought for him in their wrath, and ill would it have fared with him had they found him. Horribly frightened and seeking concealment, he turned into the house of a certain widow. She led him to a secret closet — in those days of peril there were such in many houses. "Shall I be safe here?" he asked trembling. "Oh yes, Sir," she said, "you will be quite safe, for it was here my husband hid when you sought for him and could not find him."

Ah, but he had sought for him again, and *had* found him; and now his widow, in the day of vengeance, saved the life of him who had hunted her husband to his death. Nor is that the only such story we can find in the records of Protestantism.[1]

---

[1] The following story of George Wishart, as told by John Knox, whose forerunner he was, is an equally striking instance of the "generous deed." Wishart had come to Dundee, which was being desolated by the Plague, that he might

We have spoken of the part the tender *affections of humanity* bear in all true romance. How many conflicts of the affections crowd into our minds as we recall the long, long story of the struggles of Protestantism! Take an illustration from a picture — which, whether or not it represents any single fact, certainly represents a type of innumerable facts. Most of us already know Millais' *Huguenot*, at least in engravings. It gives a visible presentment of what must have happened again and again in times of persecution; the struggle between the tenderest earthly love and the love of Him who is unseen. There stand the two figures — the Huguenot, with his earnest, steadfast face, looking tenderly down at his betrothed, while *her* beautiful face is raised up to his in intense and agonized entreaty. She is trying to bind a white scarf upon his arm, and he is taking it off. It was the token worn by the Roman Catholics in the massacre of St. Bartholomew, and she wants to make

---

comfort and minister to the despairing and panic-stricken citizens. Taking his stand on the top of the East Gateway, or Cowgate Port, he used to preach to enormous crowds; the "sick," or infected, taking their place outside, the "whole" inside the gate. "While he was spending his life," says Knox, "to comfort the afflicted, the Devil ceased not to stir up his own son the Cardinal (Beaton) again, who corrupted by money a desperate priest, named Sir John Wigton, to slay the said Master George, who looked not to himself in all things so circumspectly as worldly men would have wished. And upon a day, the sermon ended and the people departing, no man suspecting danger, and therefore not heeding the said Master George, the priest that was corrupted stood waiting at the foot of the steps, his gown loose, and his whinger drawn into his hand under his gown, the said Master George, as that he was most sharp of eye and judgment, marked him, and as he came near he said, 'My friend, what would you do?' and therewith he clapped his hand upon the priest's hand, wherein the whinger was, and took it from him. The priest abashed, fell down at his feet, and openly confessed the verity, as it was. The noise rising and coming to the ears of the sick, they cried, 'Deliver the traitor to us, or else we will take him by force;' and so they burst in at the gate. But Master George took him in his arms, and said, 'Whosoever troubles him shall trouble me; for he has hurt me in nothing, but has done great comfort both to you and to me, to wit, he has let us understand what we may fear in times to come. We will watch better.' And so he appeased both the one part and the other, and saved the life of him that sought his."

him pass for a Roman Catholic and thus to save his life. No, no! Not merely not for life — that were a little thing — but not even for the love of her will he betray his Faith, and forsake his Lord. Does not that picture make us think of the words of the Cavalier poet,

> *I could not love thee, dear, so much*
> *Loved I not Honour more?*

Only, instead of abstract, impersonal honour, we put a personal name — even the Name that is above every name.

These are the things we find so plentifully in the records of Protestantism; and they are a joy to the heart and a help to the life, for they bring us into closer communion with Him whose power and love so filled the hearts of men and women in the past, that they were able thus to do and thus to suffer for that Name's sake.

But some of us may think, "This is all very well. But after all, though Protestantism may have its heroic side, to say that it is romantic sounds strangely in our ears. We never thought of it so before; we thought it was rather the opposite — something that might indeed be right, and the best thing to believe on the whole — but still something cold, negative, and prosaic." *Cold!* — Not only do our enemies say this, but sometimes also our friends. For instance, a novelist of the present day, himself a Protestant, says of one of his fictitious characters, a Roman Catholic who married a Protestant and adopted his Faith, "She died young, perhaps she was withered by the colder creed." *Cold!* — It has stirred the hearts of men and women, not alone to a burning enthusiasm, but to that intensity of white heat which is far beyond the crimson glow of the ordinary furnace. Hear the testimony of another contemporary author, Owen Wistar, an American. He is describing the churches in a New England town — "Of these three houses of God, that one which holds the most precious flame, the purest light, is the one that treasures the holy fire that came from France (at the time of the Revocation of the Edict of Nantes). It was for liberty of soul, to lift their ardent and exalted prayer to God as their own conscience bade them and not as any man directed, that these French colonists sought the New World. No Puritan splendour of independence and indomitable courage outshines theirs. They preached a word as burning as any that Plymouth and Salem ever heard. They were but a handful, and yet so efficacious was their marvellous zeal that they became the spiritual leaven of their whole community."

The secret assemblies for worship held by Protestants in times of persecution furnish an overwhelming refutation of the charge of coldness. These assemblies were of many kinds, and held in many times and places — often in towns and cities, within closed doors. But by far the most numerous and important were held in the country — in mountains and forests, in dens and caves of the earth. Holland and Belgium in the Sixteenth century, and Bohemia, both before and after, witnessed many such. But the most remarkable were those of France, from the period of the Revocation until the eve of the Revolution, when religious toleration was granted at last. During most of that time, to attend those assemblies meant to face perils worse than death, the galleys — "those floating hells" — for the men, and cruel imprisonment for the women and children. Yet in the worst of weather, in cold and rain and sleet, when a whisper went round the district that there was to be an Assembly in such and such a place — even though it was miles away, and only to be reached by the most rugged and toilsome of paths — joy filled the hearts of the oppressed and sorrowful Protestants. What did they care about cold, hunger, weariness, or peril if only they could hear once more,

La Parole de Dieu, for which their hearts were thirsting? Peradventure also the opportunity would be given them of meeting at His Table, where truly "He was known of them in the breaking of bread." The longing to go to these Assemblies grew early, even in the hearts of the children. One little child was very eager about it, but his mother thought him far too young to go. So on the eventful night she waited until he was in bed, and as she thought asleep, and then set off with her friends. He lay still until all was quiet, and then (she had not *forbidden* him) he dressed himself again, and set off, in the cold and dark, until he came up with the party. His mother was horrified; she dreaded what might happen to him. "Oh, why did you come?" she said.

"Mother, you are going to pray to God — I know you are," he answered. "Won't you let me come too?"

She could not send him back, and as the way was far too long for his little feet, the men of the party took turns to carry him, and so he came to the assembly. He heard the prayers, the singing, and the sermon, and,

Thoughts in that young child's heart took root
Which manhood could scarcely bear.

At another Assembly a few years later he was so stirred by what he heard that, when there was a pause, he said a few words and prayed.

The people recognized a voice of power, and said he must be a pastor. In France, at that time, every Protestant pastor was, by the very fact of his calling, doomed to the gallows. And yet this lad, Antoine Court, while still almost a boy, received some kind of informal ordination, and became a pastor. He was only nineteen when there arose in his heart the thought of gathering together again the scattered flocks of the faithful Protestants in France, and arranging an ordained ministry and a settled government for "the Church of the Desert" — "the Church under the Cross" as it was most appropriately called. And he actually accomplished it. The name of Antoine Court will be ever remembered as that of the reviver and restorer of French Protestantism after the Revocation.

So much for the "*coldness*" of Protestantism. There is another thing commonly said of it — that it is *negative*, that it consists in saying this or that is not so, in exposing and denouncing error. But Protestantism in its essence is *not* negative, but positive. Primarily it is a witness *for*, and not a witness *against*; but though we certainly live by affirmations, not by negations, and "yes" is undoubtedly a better word than "no," — still, when people want to impose things upon us which would destroy our "yes," we have got to say "No" to those things. That is the way, and the only way, in which Protestantism is negative.

A great historian has said, in speaking of Queen Mary, the persecutor — who yet was not so bad as some I could mention, for she had a heart, and that heart was broken by her odious husband, Philip of Spain — "With a broken spirit and bewildered understanding she turned to Heaven for comfort, but instead of Heaven she saw only the false roof of her creed, painted to imitate and shut out the sky." Could there be a better description of Roman Catholicism than that? The only way in which we Protestants are *negative* is that we say "No" to that false roof. We will not have it — No! No! No! Down with it! Down with it, even to the ground! Let us look up straight to the glorious sky — to the face of God our Father, Christ our Redeemer, the Spirit our Sanctifier!

Another thing sometimes said, and we fear often thought, about Protestantism is that it is *prosaic*. It is not supposed, at all events, to present things in a very poetical light. But what if we find, on examination, that Protestantism is the true friend of poetry, and poetry of Protestantism? Our poets at least have thought so. Look at the record of the noblest of our English "lords of the lyre."

Shakespeare is with us, Milton is for us.

Here perhaps you object "Oh, but we cannot be sure what Shakespeare was, because Shakespeare was *everybody*." True, he *was* everybody, in the sense that he could personate everybody, could throw himself into everybody's mind by his genius. It may be said "God gave unto Shakespeare largeness of heart, like the sand that is upon the sea-shore." But, without mentioning other good reasons for assuming his Protestantism, do you remember the magnificent eulogy that he puts into the mouth of Cranmer at the baptism of Queen Elizabeth, in his drama of Henry VIII? Surely no one who sympathized with Rome would have chosen to write that — even dramatically!

Of Milton we need not speak. His Protestantism was patent to all the world.

Look now at our own Age. Look at the two great singers of the Victorian Era, both gone from us, and gone assuredly to the presence of their Lord — Robert Browning and Alfred Tennyson. You can see from the whole trend of his poems what Browning was, and here are two or three lines by way of specimen,

> . . . *Belief's fire, once for all*
> *Makes of the rest mere stuff to show itself.*

> *Why, to be Luther — what a life to lead,*
> *Incomparably better than my own.*
> *He comes, reclaims God's earth for God,*
> *Sets up God's rule again by simple means;*
> *He opens a shut book, and all is done.*

Or, those lines from the close of "Christmas Eve," when he prays that "no worse blessing" than a simple faith may "befall the Pope,"

> *Turned sick at last of today's buffoonery,*
> *Of posturings and petticoatings,*
> *Beside his Bourbon bully's gloatings*
> *In the bloody orgies of drunk poltroonery!*

Tennyson too — you know his "Queen Mary," and you cannot doubt that he puts into the mouth of Cranmer his own conviction,

> *It is but a Communion, not a mass,*
> *A holy Supper, not a Sacrifice.*

You know, too, what he thought of Rome by his splendid ballad of "The Revenge," where he speaks of "The Inquisition dogs, and the devildoms of Rome."

And he tells us, in words that may well be taken now upon our own lips, of England's,

> *Legacy of war against the Pope.*
> *From child to child, from Pope to Pope, from age to age,*
> *Till the sea wash her level with her shores,*
> *Or till the Pope be Christ's.*

May we give you also the testimony of one or two of the minor singers of our day? Some of these have witnessed well for our Protestant Faith; amongst them Elisabeth Barrett Browning, who used to be thought by many a greater poet than her husband. We do not think so now, but we think her a true poet for all that. If there is anything that people do not usually associate with romance, or poetry, it is doctrine, or dogma. They have a way of thinking of "doctrines" as if they were dry and abstract things, chiefly interesting to students of theology, and remote from ordinary feeling and experience. But this must be a mistake; for what are true doctrines but spiritual facts, and what are false doctrines but spiritual lies? And does not what is spiritual pertain to the spirit — that is, to the very highest and the very deepest within us? When poetry at her best touches with a *true* touch the things of the spirit, then indeed "deep calleth unto deep," and wonderful is the harmony in which they blend. Hear how Elizabeth Barrett Browning touches a distinctive doctrine — and one of the most distinctive doctrines — of Protestantism — the sole priesthood of Christ,

Priests, priests! — there's no such name — God's own except
Ye take most vainly. Through Heaven's lifted gate
The priestly ephod in sole glory swept,
When Christ ascended, entered in, and sate
With victor Face sublimely overwept
At Deity's right hand, to mediate,
He alone, He for ever. On His breast
The Urim and the Thummim, fed with fire
From the full Godhead, flicker with the unrest
Of human, pitiful heart-beats. Come up higher,
All Christians.

Yes, let all Christians "come up higher," and acknowledge also that Poetry is never more true to herself than when she pours out her gold, her frankincense and her myrrh at the feet of Christ.

Turning from higher themes to what falls unquestionably within the realm of romance, we will quote next the historian-poet who has given us the "Lays of Ancient Rome." Many of us will remember Lord Macaulay's spirited song of the Battle of Ivry, the great victory of the Huguenots. Have not our young hearts thrilled to the martial music of its concluding lines,

> *Our God hath crushed the tyrant,*
> *our God hath raised the slave,*
> *And mock'd the counsel of the wise,*
> *and the valour of the brave;*
> *Then glory to His holy Name, from whom all glories are;*
> *And glory to our Sovereign Lord, King Henry of Navarre!*

But since it is ever true that "our sweetest songs are those that tell of saddest thought," some of us may love, better than the tale of victory, the simple verses from the same pen that tell the story of failure and disaster —

> *O, weep for Moncontour! O, weep for the hour*
> *When the children of darkness and evil had power;*
> *When the horseman of Valois triumphantly trod*
> *On the bosoms that bled for their rights and their God.*

> *O, weep for Moncontour! O, weep for the slain!*
> *Who for faith and for freedom lay slaughtered in vain;*
> *O, weep for the living who linger to bear*
> *The renegade's shame, or the exile's despair!*

> *One look, one last look to the cots and the towers,*
> *To the rows of our vines, and the beds of our flowers;*
> *To the church where the bones of our fathers decayed,*
> *Where we fondly had deemed that our own should be laid.*

> *Alas! we must leave thee, dear desolate home,*
> *To the spearmen of Uri, the shavelings of Rome;*
> *To the serpent of Florence, the sultan of Spain;*

To the pride of Anjou, and the guile of Lorraine.

Farewell to thy fountains, farewell to thy shades,
To the song of thy youths, the dance of thy maids;
To the breath of thy gardens, the hum of thy bees,
And the long waving line of the blue Pyrenees.

Farewell and for ever! The priest and the slave
May rule in the halls of the free and the brave.
Our hearths we abandon, our lands we resign,
But, Father, we kneel at no altar but Thine.

Poets, by reason of their mystic gift, have sometimes voiced "thoughts beyond their thought," telling more than they quite knew themselves. It is doubtful if Macaulay knew how simply and how truly the leaders in that disastrous fight of Moncontour did actually look up to their Father and their God, and find comfort there. This is what happened. After the crushing defeat, Coligny and one of his most trusted councillors, L'Estrange, were borne away on litters, both wounded and both also well-nigh broken-hearted. The road was too narrow for their bearers to walk abreast. But once it widened a little, and L'Estrange asked his to move forward. Then, raising his head, he looked in the face of his chief — who returned his look — but neither of them could speak a word. At last L'Estrange turned away, his eyes filled with tears. But as he did so he said just this, *"Si est ce que Dieu est très doux"* — "So is it that God is very sweet." Coligny said afterwards that through this one brief word God Himself spoke to his heart, and restored his courage for the present and his hope for the future.

Nor have other singers and romancers disdained the themes which Protestant Faith and Protestant history afford in such abundance, though certainly in this domain "there remaineth yet very much land to be possessed."

No; our faith is neither cold, nor negative, nor prosaic. While as for the characters it has formed and the deeds it has inspired — the courage, the endurance, the self-sacrifice, the faithfulness to heavenly and to earthly love — "Unroll the records," search and read, and let them speak for themselves.

WHAT IS PROTESTANTISM I?

(THE HISTORY OF THE NAME)

True to Truth, and brave for Truth,
as some at Augsburgh were.
— E. B. BROWNING

'THESE HANDS YOU MAY CRUSH, THESE ARMS
YOU MAY SEVER.'

From *Under Calvin's Spell*
by Deborah Alcock, Author of *Crushed Yet Conquering*

II

WHAT IS PROTESTANTISM I?

(THE HISTORY OF THE NAME)

"What's in a name?" is a question that is more often asked than answered. There is a great deal in a name, for what are names but words, and what are words but servants, and very useful and important servants too? They are the servants of Thought, and Thought cannot even picture to itself how it could get on without them. It follows that, as Thought is ours, they are *our* servants. But we do not always treat these valuable servants wisely or well. We turn them into slaves; we misuse them, torture them, make them say what they don't want to say, mangle and distort them in various ways. Then, like other oppressed slaves, they are apt to avenge themselves and become our tyrants. Or else they acquire an undue influence over us and do us harm; they deceive us, they mislead us, they confuse our perceptions. Often they create in us unjust prejudices. This is the case with the word before us. Many people, by the very name of Protestantism, have been prejudiced unjustly against the thing.

Names of Churches, communities, systems, parties, and so forth, may have either of two origins, or possibly both. Sometimes they are historical, sometimes they are descriptive — the latter either truly or falsely. Socinianism, for instance, is a historic name. In the sixteenth century two men, uncle and nephew, named Socinus, denied the Divinity of Christ, and their followers were called Socinians. On the other hand, those who deny the same truth are now usually called

Unitarians. That is a descriptive name, meant to show that they believe in the Unity but not in the Tri-Unity of God. The name we have to deal with had a historic origin, and it has also a descriptive meaning. It has moreover the advantage of being a name that can be used alike by those who are Protestants and by those who are not; by the former with just pride and satisfaction; and by the latter without offence.

It must be understood at the outset that the Protestant Faith existed many ages before the Protestant name. When did the Protestant Faith begin? To answer that we must go back to the beginning of the Christian Faith itself. We must certainly go back to St. Paul, whose writings, next to the Four Gospels, have been studied, loved, and appealed to by Protestants in all ages, because he was the man who, under the guidance of the Divine Spirit, arranged and systematized for us the doctrines of our Faith. Not we ourselves alone, but even some of our candid and intelligent opponents, have linked our name with that of St. Paul. Not long ago, a friend of mine who was visiting the beautiful church of the *Tre Fontane*, dedicated to St. Paul, was told by the very courteous monk who conducted her, "St. Paul is *your* Saint, St. Peter is *our* Saint." While we do not renounce our claim upon St. Peter, we certainly do acknowledge a close and special tie to the Apostle of the Gentiles.

But while the Protestant Faith, in its substance, was certainly taught by St. Paul, the Protestant name was not given to it till nearly fifteen centuries later. We can point definitely to the time when it was given — to the year, the month, and the day, to the place also; we can even name the man who has the right, technically, to be called the first Protestant.

The name was born in the town of Spires, on the 19th of April, 1529, and the first man who had a right to bear it was John the Constant, Elector of Saxony. Martin Luther was one of his subjects. Those who know anything of the history of our Faith (and few of us know half enough of it) are sure at least to know something of the story of Martin Luther. That story certainly contains the elements of romance. We think of the poor miner's son; of the hungry boy singing for his bread in the streets of Erfurt, and of his later struggles and conflicts, so full of human interest and pathos. There is one scene that perhaps appeals to us most of all. We may call it the turning-point in his life, but it was more than that — it was the turning-point in the life of the nation, yes, even in that of the world.

No one who has been in the city of Worms can fail to remember the stately monument erected there to Martin Luther. Around the pedestal are the statues of his four predecessors, and above is the grand figure of the heroic monk himself. There he stands, as he stood once before the Emperor Charles and his courtiers and the princes and magnates of the Empire, and engraven beneath are those words of his which "the world will not willingly let die,"

> *Hier stehe Ich.*
> *Ich kann nicht anders.*
> *So hilf mir Gott! Amen.*

He had been summoned to that Diet to answer for his Faith.

He was condemned there, not by reason but by authority, and ordered to abjure his heresies, or to take the consequences. He answered that he could not so sin against God and God's commands, ending his answer with the world-famed words just quoted: "Here I stand. I can do no other. So help me God! Amen."

And the great Reformation had begun! But why had it not begun before? Others had spoken words as brave; others also had refused, for life itself, to give up the truth they knew — notably John Huss, a hundred years before, at the Council of Constance. But John Huss was burned at the stake. So were others who had made, from time to time, what may well be called "the grand refusal." Why not Martin Luther? Then, humanly speaking — and for that time — the Reformation would have been stifled in its cradle.

This was not to be. God willed it so; but in this world it is His way to work out His will by the hands of men, sometimes of one man. In this case He used a man to preserve the little flame, the survival of which just then seemed to hang upon Luther's life. That man was the Elector of Saxony, Frederick, called the Wise. He and his have good right to a place in our story; and they shall have it.

We all know that Germany was then an assemblage of states, some large and some small, which were pretty nearly independent and self-governing, only they all acknowledged the supremacy of an over-lord, the Emperor. At every vacancy the new emperor was elected by seven of the greatest of these princes, who were called on that account the Seven Electors. The emperor at this time was Charles V, who was also King of Spain; and the most illustrious of the Seven Electors was Frederick of Saxony.

A generation before, one of the Electors of Saxony was the father of twin boys, Ernest and Albert. These boys, while still in their cradle, were carried off by a daring robber named Kunz, but they were afterwards rescued by the fidelity of a servant. They grew and prospered, and at their father's death his dominions were divided between them. Ernest had the Electorate, with Wittenberg for his capital; Albert, what was called the Duchy of Saxony, and his capital was Leipzig. Ernest had the best portion of the two, and the character and ability of his successor, Frederick, increased the power and prestige of the Electorate. Each was the father of a long line of princes, which continues to this day; and each at present is represented in Europe by a crowned head.

The Elector Frederick was noted not only for his wisdom and sagacity, but also for his moral integrity. He took deep interest in Luther's teaching. He pondered "these things" in his heart. But he was a cautious man, slow to commit himself. Luther, after his brave refusal to retract, had been allowed to leave Worms in safety, as the Emperor, much to his honour, could not be persuaded to violate the safe-conduct he had given him. But he was placed under the Ban of the Empire, and the Elector, his sovereign, might be required — might be compelled almost — to give him up and let him be burned as a "heretic." *That* Frederick would not do, while he could not yet resolve to come boldly forward as his champion: it would have required not only tremendous courage, but more settled convictions than he had then. So what did he do? He had Luther carried off by force — but it was a friendly force — to the lonely castle of the Wartburg, where he was kept in safety and seclusion until the worst of the danger was over. He also protected his friends and followers.

Luther, during his ten months' stay at the Wartburg, did much beside throwing at the devil the historic ink-bottle, the stains of which, on the wall of his chamber, are, I believe, still shown to visitors. He bestowed upon his countrymen, for then and for all time, the inestimable boon of the New Testament in the language "understanded of the people." Later, with the assistance of learned friends in Wittenberg, especially of Melanchthon, he completed the translation of the whole Bible. But the Elector had not asked *his* leave to consign him to the Wartburg, and he did not ask the Elector's to return to the scene of conflict, where, for many reasons, his presence was needed.

During his stay in the Wartburg his cowl and his monk's robe had been taken from him; he had been made to pass for a layman, and called "Junker Georg" — "Squire George." In this disguise he left the castle, and travelled homewards. There is a pleasant story of his meeting, at an inn at Jena, two young Swiss, "poor scholars," who were going to study at Wittenberg, attracted by what they had heard of the new teaching there. The lads, poor and shy and timid, feared to sit down with the strange gentleman, but his genial, kindly ways soon set them at their ease. He gave them a good supper; and, with his strong sense of humour, evidently enjoyed the talk that followed about that mysterious Dr. Luther, of whom they had heard such conflicting reports, and whom they were longing to see.

Luther continued to enjoy the protection of the Elector; but the head of the Albertine House, Duke George of Saxony, was his fiercest opponent. So violent was he that when Luther was asked to go to his capital to hold a disputation, his friends were much alarmed for his safety, "Don't go to Leipzig," they said, "Duke George will be sure to kill you." Luther's answer was, "I would go to Leipzig if it were to rain Duke Georges for nine days together, and each Duke George nine times as fierce as he is." "Happily no such cataclysm of Duke Georges took place," the historian adds drily.

Meanwhile, and afterwards, the word that he spoke grew and prospered, and spread in various ways and in many places. It would not be fair to say that all the new Light came from the torch so bravely kindled by Martin Luther. We sometimes say vaguely, yet not unwisely, "Such and such a thought — or movement — is in the air." The air that in that wonderful age breathed "upon the dry bones" of the spiritually dead was surely an air from Heaven. It brought with it the unveiling of the long-hidden and neglected Word of God. This was done, first for the learned, through the Greek Testament of Erasmus, then for the common people, who through Luther for Germany, through Tyndale for England, and through other interpreters for other lands — were enabled to read in their own tongues the wonderful works of God.

But soon opposition arose, and persecution. Intensest passion was aroused. A new era of Martyrs began. There had been many martyrs before, and for the same truths; but the martyrs of the *Reformation* began now. The first to suffer were three young Augustinian monks, Esch, Voes, and Lambert, who were burned at Brussels in 1523. Their fate and their constancy inspired Luther's glorious hymn,

> *Flung to the heedless winds,*
> *Or on the waters cast,*
> *Their ashes shall be watched*
> *And gathered at the last;*
>
> *And from that scattered dust,*
> *Around us and abroad,*
> *Shall spring a plenteous seed*
> *Of witnesses for God.*
>
> *Jesus hath now received*
> *Their latest living breath,*
> *Yet vain is Satan's hope*
> *Of victory in their death.*
>
> *Still, still, though dead they speak,*
> *And trumpet-tongued, proclaim*
> *To many a wakening land*
> *The one availing Name.*

Another obscure martyr, one Leonard Kayser, who died bravely for the Faith, was lifted into eminence by Luther. "What am I," said the great Reformer, "What am I, an empty talker, beside this great doer?"

To France the Light had come early; chiefly through the teaching of Lefêvre, a Professor in the Sorbonne, the University of Paris. Martyr fires were soon kindled. The first sufferer was Jean Leclere, a wool-comber of Meaux; but his name finds no place in the crowded martyrologies of the Reformed Church, because, having destroyed an image, he was not given the option of saving his life by a retraction. So little anxious have we Protestants ever been to swell the lists of our martyrs, which nevertheless are crammed to overflowing!

Other victims followed in quick succession. In the very year when Protestantism was — not *born* but *baptized*, there was one who deserves to be remembered. A great contrast to the poor wool-comber Leclere was the brilliant, gifted young noble, Louis de Berquin, with all the prestige of his learning and the charm of his varied accomplishments. He was favoured by the King, Francis I, of France, and by the King's sister, Margaret of Valois, who herself leaned strongly to the cause of Reform. They, and other friends in high places, protected him from his enemies for six long years; but they either could not or would not do more; probably Francis would not, and Margaret could not. He was abandoned; and he went to the stake with joy, attired as if for a festival, "for," said he, "I am going this day to be presented to the King — not to the King of France, but to the King of kings." It was said of Louis de Berquin that "he would have been a second Luther, had he found in Francis a second Elector of Saxony."

To return to our theme — the name of Protestant. In the year 1526 — five years after the Diet of Worms — another Diet was held at Spires. There was much contention there about religion. The Romish party wanted the Reformers to be put down at once, and burned or otherwise slain. But, having already some of the princes on their side, they had grown too strong for that; and in the end they obtained from the Diet a fair measure of toleration.

As time went on, however, the hostility of the Romish party increased. The Emperor Charles, a bigoted Spaniard, shared it of course, and so did his brother and destined successor Ferdinand, then styled King of the Romans. After three years it became expedient to summon another Diet, which was again held at Spires, in 1529. At this Diet things went hard with the Reformers. They were outnumbered, and the persecuting spirit of their antagonists was rising. The last Diet, it was said, had given them far too much liberty — they must now be put down with a strong hand. The Emperor Charles was not present. Ferdinand, one of their greatest enemies, presided, and threw all his weight against them. The Princes and Deputies favourable to their cause maintained it stoutly, but in vain. They were the minority; and, like other minorities, they had to suffer. A decree was passed greatly curtailing the liberty given them three years before. It was doubtful whether they themselves would continue to be allowed the free exercise of their Faith, and certain that no one else might join them. All who might wish to do so in future were left exposed to the horrible rigour of the old persecuting laws.

They could not consent to *that!* Four Princes of the Empire — the Elector of Saxony, the Landgrave of Hesse, the Margrave of Brandenburgh, and the Prince of Anhalt — had now embraced the Faith, and there were besides the Chancellor of Luneburgh and the Deputies of fourteen free Imperial cities. They consulted with each other. "We are outnumbered," they said. "What are we to do? We cannot stay here. We must go home, protect our own people, and make ready for whatever may happen. And so may God help us! But we won't go home in silence. We will *protest* against this iniquitous decree."

So the great Protest was drawn up, and signed by them all. The first hand set to it was that of John, Elector of Saxony, brother and successor of Luther's protector, Frederick the Wise. The Elector John was therefore the first Protestant, in the historical acceptation of the name. On the 19th of April, 1529, the Princes and the Deputies came in to the great Hall of Spires and solemnly presented their Protest. It was their word to the Diet, to the Emperor, to the world.[2] Having done this, and

---

[2] It may be well to give, in an abridged form, the text of this truly epoch-making document. We quote it from Merle d'Aubigné's *History of the Reformation*:

"Dear Lords, Cousins, Uncles, and Friends! Having repaired to this diet at the summons of his Majesty, and for the common good of the empire and of Christendom, we have heard and learnt that the decisions of the last diet concerning our holy Christian faith are to be repealed, and that it is proposed to substitute for them certain restrictive and onerous resolutions.

"King Ferdinand and the other imperial commissaries, by affixing their seals to the last Recess of Spires, had promised, however, in the name of the emperor, to carry out sincerely and inviolably all that it contained, and to permit nothing that was contrary to it. In like manner, also, you and we, electors, princes, prelates, lords, and deputies of the empire, bound ourselves to maintain always and with our whole might every article of that decree.

"We cannot therefore consent to its repeal:

"Firstly, because we believe that his Imperial Majesty (as well as you and we) is called to maintain firmly what has been unanimously and solemnly resolved.

"Secondly, because it concerns the glory of God and the salvation of our souls, and that in such matters we ought to have regard, above all, to the commandment of God, who is King of kings and Lord of lords; each of us rendering Him account for himself, without caring the least in the world about majority or minority.

"We form no judgment on that which concerns you, most dear lords; and we are content to pray God daily that He will bring us all to unity of faith, in truth, charity, and holiness, through Jesus Christ, our Throne of Grace and our only Mediator.

"But in what concerns ourselves, adhesion to your resolution (and let every honest man be judge!) would be acting against our conscience, condemning a doctrine that we maintain to be Christian, and pronouncing that it ought to be abolished in our states, if we could do so without trouble.

"This would be to deny our Lord Jesus Christ, to reject His holy Word, and thus give Him just reason to deny us in turn before His Father, as He has threatened.

"What! We ratify this edict! We assert that when Almighty God calls a man to His knowledge, this man cannot however receive the knowledge of God! Oh! Of what deadly backslidings should we not thus become the accomplices, not only among our own subjects, but also among yours!

"For this reason we reject the yoke that is imposed on us. And although it is universally known that in our states the holy Sacrament of the body and blood of our Lord is becomingly administered, we cannot adhere to what the edict proposes against the Sacramentarians, seeing that the imperial edict did not speak of them, that they have not been heard, and that we cannot resolve upon such important points before the next council.

"Moreover" — (and this is the essential part of the protest) — "the new edict declaring the ministers shall preach the Gospel, explaining it according to the without waiting for the termination of the Diet, they rode away from the city and returned to their homes.

In this Protest two great principles were maintained. One was the supremacy of the Word of God. ". . . We are resolved, by the Grace of God, to maintain the pure and exclusive teaching of His only Word, such as is contained in the Biblical books of the Old and New Testaments, without adding anything thereto that may be contrary to it. This Word is the only truth, it is the sure rule of all doctrine and of all life, and can never fail or deceive us."

If this principle represented the duty of man to God, as speaking in His Word, the other represented the duty of man

---

writings accepted by the holy Christian Church, we think that, for this regulation to have any value, we should first agree on what is meant by the true and holy Church. Now, seeing that there is great diversity of opinion in this respect; that there is no sure doctrine but such as is conformable to the Word of God; that the Lord forbids the teaching of any other doctrine; that each text of the Holy Scriptures ought to be explained by other and clearer texts; that this holy book is in all things necessary for the Christian, easy of understanding, and calculated to scatter the darkness; we are resolved, with the grace of God, to maintain the pure and exclusive preaching of His holy Word, such as it is contained in the Biblical books of the Old and New Testament, without adding anything thereto that may be contrary to it. This Word is the only truth; it is the sure rule of all doctrine and of all life, and can never fail or deceive us. He who builds on this foundation shall stand against all the powers of hell, while all the human vanities that are set up against it shall fall before the face of God.

"For these reasons, most dear lords, uncles, cousins, and friends, we earnestly entreat you to weigh carefully our grievances and our motives. If you do not yield to our request, we PROTEST by these presents, before God, our only Creator, Preserver, Redeemer, and Saviour, and who will one day be our Judge, as well as before all men and all creatures, that we, for us and for our people, neither consent nor adhere in any manner whatsoever to the proposed decree, in anything that is contrary to God, to His holy Word, to our right conscience, to the salvation of our own souls, and to the last decree of Spires.

"At the same time we are in expectation that his Imperial Majesty will behave toward us like a Christian prince who loves God above all things; and we declare ourselves ready to pay unto him, as well as unto you, gracious lords, all the affection and obedience that are our just and legitimate duty."

Thus, in presence of the diet, spoke out those courageous men whom Christendom will henceforth denominate THE PROTESTANTS.

to man. No, they would not refuse the right hand of fellowship and of help to those who hereafter might desire to embrace the same Faith. God forbid!

Those who signed that Protest were called the Protestant, or the Protesting, Princes and Deputies. Their followers and adherents were called the Protesters, or the Protestants. So that Protest began in the world the existence of the Protestant *name*. It was no unworthy beginning, but a noble and an honourable one, of which we may be justly proud.

That is not the end of the story — it is the beginning. The Protestants returned home, as we have said — but with what prospects for the future? They had thrown down the gage of battle, and had nothing now to expect but hostility. They knew that their dominions, their sovereignty, their subjects would all be threatened. But they did not think of retreating or retracting. They thought only of defending their Faith and explaining their principles. So the Protest of Spires was followed the next year by the "Confession of Augsburg" — the Lutheran Confession of Faith, which the Churches called Lutheran still accept as their standard. The Confession was drawn up; it was to be signed — who was to sign it first? Clearly the Elector had the right to do it, if he would — but would he? He would. He took the pen in hand; but those around tried to dissuade him. "You will endanger your crown," they said.

His answer was, "God forbid you should exclude me. My crown is not so precious to me as the Cross of Christ. My crown I must leave on earth, but my Master's Cross I shall bring with me to heaven."

He meant what he said, and he had soon an opportunity of proving it. Next year, at Augsburg, there was another great Diet. The Confession was brought thither by the Princes and presented to the Emperor. Charles was a cold, reserved man; moreover, he was no linguist. Unlike the celebrated diplomatist who "could keep silence in seven languages," he, the supreme ruler of Germany, never learned more than a few words of German, and even these he seldom spoke. On one occasion the Margrave of Brandenburgh, in his eagerness to make him understand what the Confession of Faith meant for himself, knelt down at his feet and said, "Rather than abandon the Word of God, I would kneel down before your Majesty and" — drawing his hand across his throat — "and have my head cut off." The cold heart of Charles was moved for once. Stretching out his hand to arrest him, he said, "Dear Prince, not the head — not the head!" and these are said to have been the only German words he uttered throughout the Diet.

During the Diet every effort was made, every art was tried, to break the resolution of the protesting princes, and win them back to the fold of Rome. No threats of dire disaster to themselves and their subjects, no splendid offers of advancement were spared. But they stood like rocks, headed by John the Constant, whose faith and courage nothing could shake. When threatened with the loss of his Electorate, he only said, "It was God who made me Elector — me, who was not worthy of it. I throw myself into His arms, let Him do with me what seems good unto Him." Had it been demanded of him, this sovereign prince would have gone to the stake for his Faith as readily as any poor man. His son and heir, John Frederick, was equally steadfast. If the princes left Spires in a manner overborne and defeated, they went home as conquerors from Augsburgh. They had won a moral victory. They had stood the test, and shown themselves indeed "true to truth, and brave for truth." But their enemies were many and powerful, and clouds soon gathered over their prospects. Once and again they gathered, and once and again they were dispersed, or seemed to be. At length the Protestants made a League for their own defence which was called the League of Schmalkald. This was followed, after a time, by the inevitable war. Sooner or later, wherever Protestants were strong enough to fight at all and yet not the preponderating power in the State, "Wars of Religion," as they were called, were almost sure to arise. And for one simple reason. Rome had but one doom, one destiny, for all those who left her Communion and refused to return to it, and that was — *extermination*. Not in the etymological sense of the word, which means only putting beyond the frontier, but in the sense it has acquired now — absolute and universal *killing out*. She has attempted to do this wherever she has held undisputed sway; and has succeeded sometimes, as in Spain. It was considered a matter of course that "heretics" should die — and die, if possible, the death of fire. There are many more people now, I should think, who doubt that a murderer ought to be hanged than there were then who doubted that a "heretic" ought to be burned. Then what could the "heretics" be expected to do, once they became strong and numerous?

There are some good people who ask, "Is it right to go to war at all? Does not our Lord say 'Resist not evil'?" Yes, but He says it to individuals not to communities.

Every man has a right — and a right which often becomes a duty — to give up his own property, his own life even, rather than resist evil. That concerns himself; but has he also a right to sacrifice others — perchance those nearest and dearest to him — perchance the weak and helpless, who cannot fight for themselves?

If a strong man is attacked he may resist or no — he has his choice. But if he sees a woman or a child attacked, what is he to do? Is he not to resist *that* evil? "Martyrdom," it has been truly said, "is all very well for the martyrs, but little honour to those that stand by and see the stones thrown." These first Protestants could not, would not, should not, stand by and see the stones thrown, or the fires kindled, when they were strong enough to prevent it. And, as even the light of Nature taught,

> *How can man die better*
> *Than facing fearful odds*
> *For the ashes of his fathers*
> *And the temples of his gods,*
> *And for the tender mother*
> *Who dandled him to rest,*
> *And for the wife who nurses*
> *His baby at her breast?*

So at last, in the course of things, the League of Schmalkald had to be followed by the War of Schmalkald. Just before it broke out, Martin Luther was taken to the Home of Everlasting Peace. He died in 1546. John, the Constant Elector, also slept with his fathers, but his successor was as staunch a Protestant as he. It was said of him indeed that he was "more Lutheran than Luther himself." As his uncle was called "the Wise," and his father "the Constant," so he has won the honourable title of John Frederick "the Great-hearted."

The Elector of Saxony and the Landgrave of Hesse were the heads of the Protestant League and the generals of the Protestant army. It cannot be said that, as a military commander, either of them was able to cope with Charles V, perhaps the greatest general of his age. Still, things would probably have gone better with them and with their cause but for the extraordinary treachery of one who was a near relative of both, and also a Protestant in name. Luther's stout opponent, Duke George, of the Albertine line, having died childless, had been succeeded by his brother Henry, and he in turn by his son Maurice, a young man of great abilities and corresponding ambition. The Elector, who had shown him much kindness, left him, in all confidence, to guard his own dominions when he marched against the Emperor. But Maurice made peace with Charles, and having first ravaged the Electorate himself, surrendered it to him. This obliged the Elector to separate his forces from those of the Landgrave, and to march homewards. His army met that of the Emperor at a place called Mühlberg, where a battle was fought, in which the Protestants were totally defeated, and the Elector wounded and made prisoner. The captive was led up to where, flushed with victory, the Emperor Charles and his brother Ferdinand were standing together. Contrary to all the rules of chivalry, they received him with words of bitter reproach and insult. He made no answer, but turned silently away. The day was stormy, and at that moment a peal of thunder rent the sky. The wounded, defeated man raised his eyes upward: "O Thou ancient Almighty One," said he, "Thy voice telleth me Thou still livest, and hath not forsaken me." No; God indeed had not forsaken him.

The Emperor marched on to Wittenberg, the Elector's capital, which he thought would yield to him immediately; but he found the gates shut and the people prepared for a vigorous resistance. This was the work of Sybilla, the Elector's devoted wife. I suppose there was not in palace, hall, or cottage a happier domestic life than theirs. She was the sister of that highly respectable but decidedly unromantic person, Anne of Cleves, the divorced consort of our Henry VIII. The Electress Sybilla is a much more interesting figure, and not alien to our subject, if there be romance in true and constant affection. She had been a mere child, not yet fourteen, when the son and heir of the Elector of Saxony made her his bride, so that her character must have been in a great measure formed afterwards. She was a loving wife and an excellent mother, and the Court over which she presided was a model of virtue. She had now made up her mind to fight to the last for the Protestant cause and the inheritance of her husband. So she returned a firm answer to the Emperor's summons to surrender.

To overcome this unexpected and most inconvenient check to his designs, Charles took an extraordinary, not to say an outrageous step. The Elector and the Landgrave had been already put under the Ban of the Empire, and thus formally outlawed. Yet to condemn a prince, and the first prince of the Empire, to death, and that by the sentence of a court-martial, was an unprecedented, an unheard of thing to do. No matter: the court was formed, with the notorious Duke of Alva at its head, and it did the work expected of it. The sentence was pronounced — the Elector was to die.

He heard it with perfect calmness. "I understand what the Emperor is doing," he said. "I must die because Wittenberg will not surrender and I will die willingly to save their just inheritance to my children." But Sybilla had also to be reckoned with. What could anyone, in such a case, expect from the heart of a woman? Had he even laid his commands upon her not to open the gates, I think she would have done it. It *was* done, at all events; and the Emperor entered Wittenberg in triumph.

It fared hardly, after that, with the captive Elector. He was separated from all he loved; humiliated, insulted, carried about everywhere in the train of the victorious Emperor as a spectacle to grace his triumph. All his dominions, except the town of Gotha and its surroundings, were taken from him, and given to his treacherous cousin Maurice, who was invested with the Electorate in his very sight, for it happened that the windows of his prison looked out upon the Square in which the imposing ceremony took place. But none of these things moved him. God's peace was with him; and his own words tell the secret of the calm and dignified bearing that impressed all about him, even his Spanish guard. Sybilla's poignant grief for him he comforted with the thought, "All I suffer now comes upon me through the will of God, whose I am and whom I serve." And again he wrote, "Living or dying, imprisoned or free, I am still His. I am redeemed by the precious Blood of Christ, and not a hair of my head can fall to the ground without His will." That thought, "I am His," kept him calm and strong amidst trials which, to many men, would have been harder to bear than death itself. "My crown is not so precious to me as the Cross of Christ," had the father said; and the son, who parted with the crown and kept the Cross, found that the choice was good.

One consolation the captive had, during a part of his imprisonment. Lucas Cranach, the painter to whom we owe the contemporary likenesses of Luther and Melanchthon and other well-known men of the time, and who had resided at his Court, asked leave to share the captivity of his patron and his friend, and seems to have been permitted to do so for some time.

The Emperor, after his triumph, tried to impose his will, in matters of religion, upon the Empire. He decreed that all should conform to a "scheme" of his own, which included the retention of most of the Romish doctrines and practices, until a General Council could be summoned to decide upon the points in dispute. This scheme, as it was only to continue until then, was called the Interim. The return to Romish practices was opposed by the more zealous and enlightened Protestants, though many of the less advanced, or less earnest, yielded to the Emperor's authority. Charles was most anxious to gain over to his views the captive Elector — now Elector no longer, but only Duke of Saxe-Cobourg and Gotha (names very familiar to us). He offered him his liberty, if only he would express his approval of the Interim. But John Frederick knew that this would involve unfaithfulness to Him whose he was and whom he served. So he refused; and, in consequence, the rigour of his captivity was increased. Charles even went the length of depriving him of the books that had been the solace of his imprisonment.

Meanwhile his true wife Sybilla had retired to Saxe-Weimar with her little Court of friends and kinsfolk. There she lived and prayed, trying to do good to all about her, and corresponding when she could, with her captive husband. To the hymn of Luther's which she sang daily with her household, she added the verse,

> *O God, our supplications hear,*
> *For our true Lord, Thy servant dear;*
> *Maintain his steadfast faith in Thee,*
> *And in Thine own time, set him free.*

And from her own lips the cry was often heard, "O Lord, turn again my misery." God granted the prayer; and He did it by very strange means. The same Maurice who behaved so treacherously before, and nearly ruined the Protestant cause, now turned against the Emperor, his patron, and dealt him a crushing blow. Having secretly prepared an expedition, he made a sudden march upon Charles, and took him unawares, so that it was only by a hurried flight from Innsbruck, where he was at the time, that he escaped being made a prisoner. Indeed, some of Maurice's followers urged him to hurry on and he would catch the Emperor, but he answered prudently, "I have no cage for so big a bird!"

The Emperor, when he fled in haste from Maurice, still found time to give John Frederick, who was with him, his liberty. Had he not done so, Maurice on his arrival would no doubt have set him free; but we are not surprised to learn that John Frederick, though he might forgive his treacherous kinsmen, still preferred to receive the boon from other hands. Most of all, he desired to owe it to the publicly expressed will of Germany, and for this purpose he accompanied the Emperor in his flight, and came with him to Augsburgh. There a "pacification" was presently concluded, and he was set free.

His last interview with the Emperor was very friendly. Kind words were spoken, for Charles had learned both to respect and to like his captive.

The Duke went to Weimar; his new home. Everywhere, as he passed through the country, he was welcomed with rejoicing. Children met him singing hymns; flowers were strewn before him; the people from the towns came to do him honour. It was a triumphal progress. The conquered was treated everywhere as if he had come home a conqueror. He could not understand it; he said, with tears in his eyes, "Who am I, that God should honour me thus?" Sybilla's joy may be imagined; but at first it was too much for her feeble frame, and at the long-desired meeting she fainted. It was but for a brief season, after all, that these two, who had been sundered so painfully, were left together — upon earth. Sybilla, had been long in failing health; and John Frederick, though little past fifty, was prematurely worn and aged. Just eighteen peaceful months were given them, like a calm, fair sunset after a stormy day. Then both together "felt the low call of death." Though himself very ill and weak, he was able to keep his place beside her to the end, and to witness the holy joy with which she welcomed her summons, saying she "knew it was but the journey to the heavenly country." Only twelve days afterwards he followed her there; and thus "in death they were not divided."

John Frederick the Great-hearted could not have a better epitaph than the few words in which Roger Ascham, the tutor of Lady Jane Grey, summed up his character: "In all his fortunes he was reverenced of his enemies, desired of his friends, loved of all men."

Is it not true that each one of us,

Boasts two soul sides —
One to face the world with,

And one,

turned toward the unseen, looking Godwards, and never really seen save by Him? — like the unknown side of the moon with its "Silent silver lights and darks undreamed of."

On each side life writes an inscription. If on the side looking Godwards there is written, "*I am His,*" I think that on the other side, where the world can see and read it, there will generally be found another inscription — something like the character described by Roger Ascham.

In the *Cambridge Modern History* — not given to over-praise — the Elector John Frederick of Saxony is styled "the most blameless of men." Does not this recall to our memory the honoured name of another Prince, who, in our own day, wore "the white flower of a blameless life"? Prince Albert of Saxe-Cobourg and Gotha, "the noble father of our kings to be," was the lineal descendant and representative of John Frederick of Saxony, the man who lost — *lost nobly* — the higher place and dignity of Elector. The Electorate remained in the Albertine line, which is now represented by the King of Saxony. That was, in the sixteenth century, the line that *succeeded*. But what of the line that *failed*, the Ernestine? How is *that* line represented now? Here, amongst ourselves, and doubly — both through his father and his mother — in our present honoured sovereign, King Edward VII, on whose dominions the sun never sets.

Well may we say and sing, and not only say and sing, but pray with full hearts,

GOD SAVE THE KING

After the atempted murder of George Wishart
From *No Cross, No Crown: A Tale of the Scottish Reformation*
by Deborah Alcock, Author of *Crushed Yet Conquering*

WHAT IS PROTESTANTISM II?

(THE MEANING OF THE NAME)

The cloud of WITNESS solemnly advances,
Widening as each clarion voice is hushed in death below.
— From *The Cloud of Witness*

From *The King's Service: A Story of the Thirty Years War*
by Deborah Alcock, Author of *Crushed Yet Conquering*

III

WHAT IS PROTESTANTISM II?

(THE MEANING OF THE NAME)

We have spoken of the circumstances which attended the assuming — or rather the receiving — of the name of Protestant. We are going to speak now of the meaning of the name. A name which is historical in its origin does not usually have an appropriate meaning apart from its history; while even the names which are given or assumed for their meaning are sometimes singularly inappropriate. We do not find Methodists particularly methodical; and Quakers have been seldom known to quake — even before very serious dangers. But with regard to this word Protestant: we have found that its history is one we can remember with pride and thankfulness, and I think we shall also find that its meaning is both honourable and appropriate.

It is indeed a noble name. We venture to think there is only one which is higher and grander. That name also is both historic and descriptive. It is the best and dearest name by which any of us can be called — the name of Christian. We claim for the name of Protestant a place, in our hearts and on our lips, second only to that.

No doubt you know already that Protestant means *witness*. It is derived from the Latin word *testis* — a witness. Tes*tant* is witness*ing*. A Protestant then is a witness, or a person witnessing. It is a word that often occurs in Scripture. Where we have *witness* in our English Version, in the Vulgate, or Latin Version, which is used by Roman Catholics, the word is *testis*, or one of its variations. It is the word applied to the

55

Apostles, the first witnesses of Christ — to St. Stephen, to the "great cloud of witnesses," to our Lord Himself in the first chapter of Revelation; and later on, in a passage most significant for us, to the mysterious "Two Witnesses" of whom the voice of prophecy tells us. But there is a prefix to the root. We do not call ourselves Testants, but Pro-testants. Here is an instance of what in course of time very often happens to words. The current and popularly accepted meaning has wandered somehow from the original and derivative one. If "the man in the street," who seems now to be considered a sort of universal referee, is asked, "What is a Protestant?" he will probably answer, "One who protests against the doctrines of Rome," or "against the errors of Rome," according to his point of view. True, so far as it goes; but by no means all the truth, or even the greater part of the truth. The prefix *pro* does not mean against, it means *for*. During the South African war we heard a great deal of certain people who were called pro-Boers; were they people particularly distinguished by their hostility to the Boers — dead against them, so to speak? And when we talk of the "pros and cons" of any matter, do not we assume that the "pros" are the things for it and the "cons" the things against it? To protest, therefore, means literally and derivatively to witness *for*.

Yet it is not difficult to see how, both in ordinary use and in this special use of it, the word has come in the popular mind to change its meaning. If we stir ourselves up to witness against anything, it is generally because that thing is opposing, interfering with, something we value. We only care to witness *against* what is contrary to that which we witness *for*. But then, as time goes on, we often come to think more and more of what we witness against and less and less of what we witness for — a thing much to be regretted.

It will be well for us to bring back our word Protestant to its original meaning, and fix our thoughts upon the things we are witnesses *for*, in place of the things we are witnesses *against*. *Whose* witnesses are we? God's witnesses. *For what*? For several things.

We shall name first that to which the first historical Protestants gave the foremost place in their Protest — the Word of God, "seeing," said they, "that there is no sure rule for doctrine and for life except the Word of God." Thus Protestants are called to witness for the inspiration and the authority of the Word of God. On this point the articles of the Reformed and Protestant Church of England speak with no uncertain sound. The Sixth Article declares that we are not called upon to believe anything that cannot be proved from Holy Scripture, and that Holy Scripture is to be the rule both of our teaching and our life.

Another thing we are called to witness for is — Truth. What do we mean by Truth? There are two meanings we may give to it. When we use long words we speak of truth objective and truth subjective. But when we want to speak more simply we say, "Truth means the thing that is true; and that is what we have got to find out as far as we can." That is Truth objective. Whatever is presented to us we must examine, and see if it represents reality and fact — if it is truth and not a lie. But sometimes we say instead, "When we have found the truth we must ourselves be true to it." That is Truth subjective. We must not only believe what is true, but also be true to what we believe. The two things are very alike, but they are not the same. When Galileo came to believe that the earth turned round the sun, he had the truth, objectively. He knew the fact as it was. But when, under the terrors of the Inquisition, he denied that fact, and said that the sun turned round the earth, he was not truthful, not true himself to the truth he knew.[3]

---

[3] That Galileo nevertheless was wrong is clear from Scripture since God created the earth as the centre of the universe. Not science but God's Word should be our guide. See also on this fact, Philip Stott, *Vital Questions*, pp. 85-106. It is unfortunate that the author uses this example. — Editor

In these two ways — seeking honestly to find out what is true, and when we have found it being true to it in word and act — Protestantism bears witness to truth. Romanism does not do so. She will very readily, even gladly, allow people to believe what she thinks edifying, what she thinks helpful, what she thinks pious — "a pious opinion" she calls it, whether it be true or no. "Oh," she says, "it will do people good — let them believe it. Why not?"

For instance, there is a legend that one of the martyrs, St. Denys, who had his head cut off, took if up afterwards in his hands and walked away with it. Romanists say: "Whether that happened or not, it is very nice for the people to believe it." *We* say: "Did that thing really happen? Did that man really walk away with his head in his hands? We are sure he did *not*, as a matter of fact; and so we will have none of it!" And, having tried to find what is true, we will also try, if God gives us His grace, to be true to the truth we have found. Marvellously indeed has He given of His grace to men and to women — yes, and to children, too — enabling them to refuse, for any fear of punishment or any hope of honour or reward, to say with their lips the things their hearts could not believe.

We are witnesses also, by virtue of our Protestantism, for another thing — we are witnesses for Freedom. Everyone who has studied history in anything like an impartial spirit must acknowledge the immense services Protestantism has rendered to the cause of freedom. Look at the nations of Europe as they stand now, and see what Protestantism has done for those who accepted it, in making them free, in making them great, and in making them prosperous. See also what those have missed who rejected it. The reason is obvious; for that principle, "We will seek the truth, we will find the truth, we will hold to the truth," plants in the mind of every man who receives it the living seed of freedom. It imparts a strength which all the material forces of tyranny cannot overcome. To take one out of many illustrations — Palissy, the Huguenot potter, was a man of genius, and he gave an impulse to his art that lasts to this day. His works may still be seen, and his life may still be studied with pleasure. For he was a man who feared God, and could not be moved from the truth he had embraced, even in the darkest days of persecution. In the Massacre of St. Bartholomew he was spared, probably by favour of the King, who admired his works and liked him personally. But he was put in prison, where the King himself visited him and urged him to change his religion, "If you will not become a Catholic," he said, "I am very sorry, but I shall be compelled to let your enemies have you."

"Then I am stronger than your Majesty," returned the brave Huguenot, "because no one on earth, not even you, can compel me. I will not change my religion."

Truly has it been said, "He who can die cannot be compelled." Thus in every country where Protestant faith prevailed there arose a set of men who, because they could die, could not be compelled; and through them the nation's freedom was won, or maintained.

We are witnesses, then, for Truth and for Freedom. But we do not stop there. Had we been fighting only for abstract principles, however grand or precious, our battles would never have been won. The centre of Protestantism is not a principle, not a power, not a doctrine, but a Person. In its innermost essence Protestantism is witness for *Christ*. Let this never be forgotten, let it be taken close to our hearts and held there forever. We are witnesses for Christ, for the power of Christ, for the love of Christ, for the sole claim of Christ upon our obedience, our allegiance, and our love. No one — no thing — shall stand between us and Him — no person, however venerated — no system, however splendid; no organization, however ancient or imposing. Especially we are witnesses for the finished work of Christ as our only Saviour. We know that what is usually considered the cardinal doctrine of Protestantism is the doctrine of justification by faith. It was of this Luther became the champion, and it was this which he called "the article of a standing or a falling Church." But what does it mean? We are saved by faith indeed, but faith in itself has no power to save. It is only a link uniting us to Him who saves. Justification by faith means justification by Christ — by trusting Him, following Him, *having* Him. Faith in itself is nothing — Christ is all. That is what Protestantism means — Christ is all. As one of our martyrs said in the fire, crying it out again and again in his dying agonies: "None but Christ! None but Christ!" That is the centre word of Protestantism — "None but Christ." As long as we hold to that we live, we grow, we triumph. Once let that go, and all goes.

There is something more to be said about the word Protestant. We have spoken of its derivation from the Latin *testis*, which means witness. But what is its Greek equivalent? What is the Greek word for witness? I think we all know that. There are two places in our English Authorized Version of the Bible where the Greek word is retained. In Acts 22:20 Paul speaks of "Thy martyr Stephen," and in Rev. 2:13 Christ Himself calls Antipas "My faithful martyr." *Martyr*, that is the Greek word. Everywhere, in the New Testament, where the English word "witness" is used, it is in the original "martyr." In the eleventh chapter of Revelation the "two Witnesses" are in the Greek δυσὶ ωάυσί. And in the majestic opening chapter of the same Book, One greater than all these, even He to whom they all bore witness, is Himself called "the true and faithful Martyr."

In our modern use of it, which dates almost from the beginning of the Church's history, the word "martyr" has acquired a special and distinctive meaning. It is reserved for those witnesses who have given up their lives, and sealed their testimony with their blood. In a very close and peculiar way this meaning links it with our subject. Protestantism has been emphatically the creed of the martyrs. This is a fact not half — not a hundredth part — so well known as it ought to be.

Most of us, when we think of martyrs at all, turn back instinctively to the early Christians. This is very natural. The champions of our faith, who kept its light alive in the first ages amidst the darkness of heathenism, ought indeed to be much remembered by us who enter into their labours. Their names we honour; the records of their faith and patience we carefully preserve. I wonder which of these martyr stories is the dearest to your hearts? To mine there is none so dear as the splendid witness of the aged Polycarp — possibly the very "angel of the Church of Smyrna," to whom our risen Lord addressed the words, "Be thou faithful unto death." When commanded to blaspheme Christ, or die, you remember his noble answer, "Eighty and six years have I served Him, and He has never wronged me; how then shall I blaspheme my King who has saved me?" The Master said to the servant, "Be thou faithful." The servant answered, "How can I but be faithful to my faithful Lord?" And we may be very sure the Lord received him with His grand "Well done, good and faithful servant!" *

Beautiful stories like this we find in the records of the early Church. But we must remember that after only three hundred years Christianity became the religion of the Roman Empire, and — save for the short reaction under Julian — Pagan persecution ceased entirely. During those three centuries ten persecutions are usually reckoned, but some of them were short and partial. Nor was the "world" of the Roman Empire at all so extensive as the "world" of modern Europe.

But to anyone who undertakes the labour — too sadly neglected — of searching the crowded records of Protestant martyrology, the number of the witnesses grows — and grows — and grows — until it becomes absolutely overpowering.

They are, literally, "like the stars for multitude," not merely the stars seen by the naked eye, but the stars discovered by the telescope. And when you have resolved into single stars all of these that you can so resolve, then you will find the cloudy nebulæ baffling you still.

It is hard to give anything like an adequate idea of this so great cloud of witnesses; but, by way of making some approach to it, we will carry on the symbol of the stars, remembering that "one star differs from another star in glory." They differ in "magnitude," astronomers say, but the magnitudes are apparent, not real. We hear of stars of the first, second, third magnitude, and so on; but that does not mean that those which look the largest and brightest to us are necessarily so in reality, only that they appear so, because we see them more plainly. There, too, the illustration holds good. *We* cannot tell, amongst the martyrs, which may be really "the greatest in the kingdom of heaven" — only God can do that; but we cannot fail to notice various degrees in the brightness with which they shine upon us through the darkness of the past.

There are a few stars of the first magnitude whose names every one knows, or ought to know; and there were a few martyrs who would have been great men in any case, and have found a place in history, even in what is called secular history. Amongst Englishmen, Cranmer, Ridley, and Latimer were sure to be remembered. And there is another name which I mention with the deepest reverence, a name which is known to every one of us, and which ought to be known to every man, woman, and child who can read the English language — the name of William Tyndale, the translator of the Bible, a man of real genius, as is shown by his matchless rendering of the matchless words of Scripture. Though it is not his version that we use now, yet our Authorized Version, which has been founded upon his, retains much of his language, and, deeply imprinted, the "very form and pressure" of his mind. Through this magnificent work he has influenced every one of us, and more than that, every one of the millions who read and love their English Bible. We may call *him* indeed a star of the first magnitude.[4]

There are many other martyrs of Protestantism about whom, although in the world's sense we can scarcely call them great men, we yet know a great deal, and a great deal that is extremely interesting. These include many of our English martyrs, and not a few of those of other countries. We know their books, their letters, many things about their lives, sometimes even minor details — traits of character, of personal appearance, of daily habit — which make them real to us, and not mere shadows, about their deaths we have often quite full and circumstantial information. The one I shall take for an instance, John Frith, may be truly called a "heritor of unfulfilled renown," for he was cut off early. He spent just as many years on earth as our Lord Himself did — thirty-three. But he gave such promise of future greatness that, had he lived, his name would no doubt have become famous. That was not to be; but already he had assisted Tyndale in his translation of the New Testament and moreover a trace of his hand remains to us still in our English Prayer Book. The concluding words of the Rubric at the end of the Communion Service, commonly called *the black Rubric,* are from the pen of John Frith.

---

[4] We cannot refrain from quoting in this connection the magnificent tribute paid to the English Bible by a person no less eminent than Cardinal Newman: "Who will not say that the uncommon beauty and marvellous English of the Protestant Bible is not one of the great strongholds of heresy in this country? It lives in the ear like a music that can never be forgotten, like the sound of church bells which the convert hardly knows how he can forego. Its felicities often seem to be almost things rather than words. It is part of the national mind and the anchor of national seriousness. The memory of the dead passes into it. The potent traditions of childhood are stereotyped in its verses. The power of all the griefs and trials of man is hidden beneath its words. It is the representative of his best moments, and all that has been about him of soft and gentle, and pure and penitent and good, speaks to him forever out of his English Bible."

We come now to those whom we may call stars of the third magnitude, about whose lives we do not know very much, though we have fairly ample, sometimes very ample, accounts of their deaths. Leaving England for a while, we shall take our example here from one of the multitudinous martyrs of France. This martyr suffered very late in the history of his country — later than most people suppose any martyrs suffered at all — in the middle of the eighteenth century, that so-called age of enlightenment and of reason. Yet even in that age it was a capital crime in France to be a Protestant pastor, to perform baptisms or marriages, or to administer the Holy Communion not according to the ritual of the Church of Rome. Every pastor took his office at the risk of his life; his very Ordination was a death sentence. Yet there was a regularly ordained Protestant ministry, and candidates for the office were never wanting. One of these pastors, Majal Désubas, was a young man, full of zeal and love and in consequence much beloved. His preaching made a great impression. But at the age of twenty-six he was arrested, and knew of course that he would be doomed to die. He was to be taken from the midst of his own people to a distant place, Montpellier, to be tried and executed. But his people loved him with that intense and passionate love we spoke of in our first Talk. Their hearts were moved to the depths — they *could* not let him die. They were strong men — brave men — and they vowed they would save him yet. They could do it; for in that district they were more numerous than the Roman Catholics, not to speak of the *gens d'arme* and the soldiers. They surrounded Vernoux, the town where he was, and made an unsuccessful effort to reach him, which cost some lives. Not discouraged, they were going to try again. He heard of it; and he said within himself,

> *These shall never die for me,*
> *Life-blood weighs too heavily;*

And I could not sleep in grave
With the faithful and the brave
Piled around and over me.

So from his prison he found means to write to his friends, praying them to give it up; and saying for himself that he was "very tranquil, and quite resigned to the will of God."

That letter did the work, aided by the prayers and exhortations of two other persecuted pastors who were among the people in disguise. No more blood was shed, and Désubas went to his death with joy. It is said that the judge — a stern man, and very hostile to the Protestants — could not refrain from tears when he pronounced his death sentence. And when, on the scaffold, he "trod the last steps that separated him from the living, immortal Christ," Protestants and Roman Catholics wept together. It is added by the historian that the Roman Catholics congratulated the Protestants on the credit their martyr had done them! His own people celebrated his name, and preserved his story, in artless, pathetic ballads, which passed from lip to lip, and from heart to heart, and are not forgotten yet. One stanza may be quoted, for the simple sweetness of its melody, which lingers on the ear,

Lubac n'est plus à plaindre,
Il est hors du danger;
Il n'a plus rien à craindre,
Ni rien à desirer.

But we must hasten on. There are stars of still lesser magnitude — lesser, perhaps, only because we know less about them. They are a great multitude; far more numerous — incomparably more numerous — than the martyrs whose histories we know, are those of whom we know nothing except their names; and then there are those even whose names we do not know — names, indeed,

> *On earth unknown,*
> *But Jesus bears them on His heart,*
> *Before the eternal Throne.*

It has been said of such as these,

> *They lived unknown*
> *Till persecution dragged them into fame,*
> *And chased them up to heaven.*

True, indeed, persecution "chased them up to heaven;" but it was beyond the power even of persecution to "drag them into fame." Fame has no room upon her scroll for such a multitude. And yet, just a gleam of light falls here and there upon some of these obscure names and lights them up — as in looking at a distant field, you sometimes see a sunbeam flash upon a bit of broken glass or a stone, and make of it a little sun.

Take an instance or two. One of the women martyrs of France — and there were a great many — was going to the stake. A crowd of the poor and destitute whom she had been wont to succour followed her, weeping. One poor woman sobbed out, "You will never give me alms any more." "Yes, once more," said the martyr; and stooping down, she took off her own shoes and gave them to her.

Here is another. It is of the proto-martyr of Protestantism in Spain, Francesco Romano, a victim of the Inquisition. He was bound to the stake: the fire was kindled, the flames arose. At that last moment those around him thought he made a sign as if he would recant, and tried, in mistaken kindness, to pull him out of the fire. *"Did you envy me my happiness?"* said he.

My happiness! Nothing is more wonderful than the happiness — the joy — God gave to those witnesses for Him even in the midst of their sufferings. Once and again this comes before us, sometimes in the strangest ways. A French martyr, an old man of seventy-two, was broken on the wheel — a peculiarly horrible form of death, much more lingering and protracted than the death of fire. His wife — brave woman! — stood beside him. He looked at her and said, "Though you see my bones broken to fragments, yet is my heart filled with ineffable joy!"

In searching out and studying the voluminous records of those who have suffered for Christ, there must be pain — much pain — from which our timid spirits shrink away. But the pain is more than compensated by the marvellous revelations that come to us of the power and the love that sustained them throughout all. How they help us, these heroes of the Faith, in the circumstances, the sorrows, the conflicts, of our own lives! We say to our hearts: "He helped *them* in such terrible straits; can He not help me also — even me — in the far lesser trials of my life?" Then, in that sweet sense of communion, the glad words rise from heart and lip,

There is a multitude around
Responsive to my prayer,
I hear the voice of my desire
Resounding everywhere;

But the earnest of eternal joy
In every prayer I trace,
I see the likeness of the Lord
On every patient face.

How oft, in still communion known,
Those spirits have been sent
To share the travail of my soul,
Or show me what it meant!

But even beyond what we may call the nebulæ, the multitude of witnesses for Christ whose names only, or whose very names even, have not been preserved, there remains another great multitude who perished in general massacres — those massacres of "heretics," of which that of St. Bartholomew is the most famous, though by no means the only one. We dare not give to all these thousands of victims the sacred name of martyrs; that would be to lower, perhaps even to profane it. For it is the Faith that makes the martyr; and none but God can know how many, amongst those "multitudes of the slain" sent suddenly into His presence, passed in there willingly for His sake. Some did so, as we know; Coligny, for instance, was certainly "a martyr both in will and in deed."

Still less should we think of counting those who fell in the wars of Protestantism. They do not come into our reckoning as *martyrs*, though a goodly number may find a place in our roll of heroes who "waxed valiant in fight, and turned to flight the armies of the aliens." Of these Gustavus Adolphus, the Lion of the North, is a conspicuous example. And some rays of the true martyr spirit have shone out even upon battlefields. Such was that of the Scottish soldier of Protestantism, who lay on the field wounded and helpless when the camp followers came to strip the dead. Finding him alive, they stabbed him again and again. He raised himself, and shouted with his last breath, "Were every hair on my head a man, I would die all those deaths for Christ and for His cause!" That man had the heart of a martyr.

It is hard to turn from these records of faith and patience to meet the objections of adversaries, sometimes also of ignorant or indifferent friends. They bid us remember that the cruelty and intolerance have not always been on one side and the courage and endurance on the other. One sometimes hears, one sometimes even reads, such a statement as this: "Oh, yes, Catholics have burned Protestants, and Protestants have burned Catholics." That Protestants have killed Roman Catholics is undeniable. That they killed them in times of war goes without saying and the sin is altogether with those that made the wars. They have killed them also in times of peace, sometimes in righteous retribution for manifest crimes, or in just self-defence; sometimes also, being fallible human beings, in revenge or in panic — often most well-grounded panic; and sometimes — seeing that the millions of men who called themselves Protestants must have had amongst them a proportion of bad men — from the motives and the passions which actuate such at all times. But those Roman Catholics who have been — knowingly and intentionally — *burned* by Protestants are very hard to discover. Personally, I have been looking for them these many years. And I think I have found them at last — in company with those men in buckram suits whom that redoubtable knight and hero Sir John Falstaff boasted he had slain.

Here someone interposes — I have heard the question, and marked the air of finality and of triumph that accompanied it, *"Who burned Servetus?"* We bow our heads, and plead guilty to the charge. Not, indeed, that,

> *Calvin, for the rest,*
> *Made bold to burn Servetus,*

as is usually said. Calvin, on the other hand pleaded for a mitigation of his sentence. Still, undeniably, he was burned by Protestants, and burned for his religious opinions. But he was not a Roman Catholic; he was a Unitarian, and more than that, he was a Pantheist. He avowed his belief that all that existed — even the devil himself — was a part of God. He had been actually condemned for his heresies by the Inquisition of Vienne to be burned in slow fire, but he escaped to Geneva. The agents of the Inquisition pursued him thither and demanded his surrender. The magistrates of Geneva gave him his choice — to go back to France, or to remain with them and be judged by their own laws. He chose the latter; so that the Protestants only carried out — and with a shade less of horror — the sentence already pronounced by the Roman Catholic Inquisition!

But none the less it was a crime, as no Protestant in the world now attempts to deny. No, we acknowledge and regret it. Protestants have just erected, in the city that witnessed his death, a handsome monument to Michael Servetus, in the inscription upon which they confess and deplore the sin of their ancestors.

And yet it is with thankfulness that we Protestants name the name of Michael Servetus. We do not thank God for his *fate*, but we do thank God with all our hearts for his *fame*. While, as it has been said, not persecution, not martyrdom even, can drag into fame the innumerable victims of Rome, who has not heard of Michael Servetus, the man whom the Protestants burnt in Geneva? His mournful celebrity is our vindication. If the victims of Protestantism had been more numerous, they would be less remembered.

It comes in the end to a question of proportion. A robe already black you may steep in ink without altering its appearance. But let one drop of ink fall upon a robe of white, and every beholder throws up his hands with the cry, "Oh, what a horrible stain!" But it is really the blackness of the black robe which is horrible — appalling. No one who has not gone into it — even a little way can guess how the horror grows and deepens in the soul as record after record is unfolded, each, as it seems, more frightful than the last, until finally imagination sinks outwearied, and we cry, "No more! — no more! Were they men who did these things, or were they demons?[5]

No; they were not demons — not *all* demons. Sometimes — alas! too rarely — a gleam of light crosses the gloom, some trait of mercy and pity, some touch of our common humanity. Even after the Massacre of St. Bartholomew there was at least one man, and he a bigoted Roman Catholic, who had the grace to die of the horror of it; and the names of the few who bravely ventured to disobey the Royal command to carry out the same measures in other parts of the kingdom, are recorded to their honour. There are still better things sometimes. More than once has a persecutor, like St. Paul, embraced the faith he tried to destroy. And in other cases, where we cannot say there has been repentance unto life, there has at least been genuine human remorse, and very terrible remorse too. Every one has

---

[5] Read in this connection an extract from a letter of Sir James Stephen, author of *Essays in Ecclesiastical Biography*. "When I am told, that Alexander VI, or Innocent III, or John XXIII was the Vicar of Christ upon earth, I am constrained by the indestructible logic of my mind to disbelieve it, even though the chain which connected that opinion with inspired sentiments of Holy Writ was composed of what would seem links of adamant. So of the Christianity of the persecutors in France, Spain and Portugal, Italy, Southern Germany, or the Netherlands. . . . Did the priests or priestesses of Egypt, or Paphos, ever perpetrate such guilt? Did Domitian ever commit against the early Christians offenses to be compared with those which the see of Rome, and her ministers and agents, committed from age to age against those whom they regarded as erring Christians? The [Roman] Catholic Church, you admit, has something about her which provokes the very utmost of abhorrence in some. What is that something? Is it not blood-guiltiness of a kind and of an amount, of which the records of the civilized world have no other example?" There are other testimonies to the same effect which might well be quoted — but we forbear.

heard of the terrors and agonies that shadowed the deathbed of the miserable king who, though he was by no means the most guilty of the actors in the St. Bartholomew tragedy, was yet the man by whom it was decreed and ordered. Yet even here there falls a ray of light. Charles had a Huguenot nurse, Philippe Richarde, who had cared for him in his infancy, and to whom he was sincerely attached. He had taken pains to keep her in safety during the massacre, and she was with him to the end of his brief, unhappy life. We are told that she found him one night in an agony, weeping and bewailing "the murders — the bloodshed." "I am lost!" he cried — "I am lost!" She soothed him tenderly, and bade him trust to the mercy of God, saying that if he repented God "would cover his sins with the mantle of His Son's righteousness, and not impute them unto him." When, a little later, he had received the last offices of his Church, and his weary, sin-stained soul was actually passing, it would seem as if he thought of the message of mercy, for he was heard to murmur faintly, "If Jesus, my Saviour, should number me amongst His redeemed!" Thrice over he said the words, and then he spoke no more. God knows the rest. In His hand are the spirits of all flesh, and He is very pitiful and of tender mercy.

Let our eyes be ever toward Him, and let us ever remember our high calling as His witnesses. We have indeed to witness against that which is false, against that which dishonours His name, distorts His truth, and degrades His service. But our witness *against* will be powerful and prevailing only so far as it is the outcome of our witness *for*. It is in witnessing for the Word of God, for truth, for freedom, and above all for Christ, that we shall be more than conquerors hereafter, and that even here we shall be clothed with that joy of the Lord which has been in all ages the strength of His true witnesses, His faithful martyrs.

THE LONG STORY OF THE AGES

Hear ye not the voices singing down the ages,
Echoing still the message, though the task be done?
— From *The Cloud of Witness*.

'UPON ADVENTURE BOUND LIKE A YOUNG KNIGHT-ERRANT.'

See p. 242.

From *Crushed Yet Conquering: A Story of Constance and Bohemia*
by Deborah Alcock, Author of *The Spanish Brothers*

IV

THE LONG STORY OF THE AGES

The long story of the ages, looked at from the point of view we wish to present, is not very easy to tell. Our motto bids us "hear the voices singing down the ages," yet at first it seems to most of us as if there were no voices at all to hear, or at least as if they were but few and faint. But if we go on listening patiently, it is not the silence which we come to find perplexing. It is the multitudinous murmur which begins to oppress us, voices low and loud, voices sad — yes, and voices joyful too — moans of pain, cries of anguish, passions of prayer, songs of triumph — all, all crowd around us, until we think of George Eliot's words about "the roar that lies on the other side of silence." On the other side of the silence of our ignorance and our forgetfulness there is that roar from all the past.

The story of the Reformation is not the story of Protestantism, though it is sometimes confounded with it. It is but a single chapter of it, though a very crucial and momentous chapter. That which the name signifies existed, as we have said, long before the name, and is not ended — nor like to be ended yet. Taken in its Greek form of witness unto death, the martyrs of Protestantism began long before the Reformation, and continued long after it. We have all heard the common taunt of the Romanist, "Where was your Church before Luther?" but I fear we are not always quite ready with an answer. Nevertheless we could easily give a dozen; but one will suffice for the present.

When Luther lay in his cradle — no, before he was born — there were already in Europe two protesting Churches — "visible Churches," "where," according to the definition of the Church of England in her Nineteenth Article, "the pure Word of God [was] preached and the Sacraments duly administered" — two *protesting* Churches, but not two *reformed* Churches. One is the ancient Church, protesting but not reformed, of the Waldenses or Vaudois; the other is the reformed and protesting Church of the United Brethren of Bohemia and Moravia, commonly called Moravians. They both continue unto this day.

When did the work of protesting against the growing errors and superstitions of the Church actually begin? That is a question difficult to answer; and moreover there is another which should be dealt with first. We cannot see the stars till the light has faded — when did the clear light of apostolic teaching begin to fade in the professing Church? We know it was a very gradual process. After the apostolic sun had set, the slow Northern twilight lingered long, while, scarce perceptibly, the darkness deepened. Here and there, now and then, as errors and superstitions crept in, good men arose and protested.

There were individual witnesses from very early times; but it would seem that the first organized revolt against the growing superstitions of the Church was that of a group called Paulicians. They arose out of the Eastern, not the Western, Church. About A.D. 653 a Syrian deacon, who had been in captivity, recovered his liberty, and set out to return home. He passed through the town of Samosata, where an Armenian, named Constantine, took him into his house and showed him kindness. He was grateful; and when they parted he gave Constantine what was probably the only treasure he had with him, a copy of the New Testament. Constantine had never seen the book before. He studied it with avidity, and soon a strange new light broke upon his soul. The writings of St. Paul seem to have been the chief source of his illumination; and as far as we can gather from our scanty information, which comes to us only through his enemies, it would seem as if he found his way to our Protestant faith.

What he believed for himself he taught to his friends; and they passed on the new light eagerly. So devoted were they to the Epistles of St. Paul, that they called themselves by the names of his followers, such as Sylvanus and Timotheus; and thus it was that friends and foes came to give them the name of Paulicians. Their teaching spread and grew, and then persecution began. After a considerable time Constantine was arrested, tried, and condemned to be stoned for his heresies. This was under the Byzantine Emperor, who sent an officer, high in authority, to superintend the execution. But this officer, whose name was Simeon, when he witnessed the faith and patience of the martyr, and heard of his doctrine, desired to know more. The result was that he himself stepped into the place of Constantine, and became the second leader of the Paulicians.

It is said that Simeon, full of faith and zeal, continued to preach and to evangelize for twenty-seven years. Then he too found a martyr's death, his stake being planted on the spot where Constantine had perished.

But the Paulicians grew and multiplied. In course of time its adherents became so numerous that, when persecuted, they united, and fought to defend themselves. The result was a bloody struggle, in which they were defeated, and finally massacred, or dispersed. They existed no more as a body, but many survivors seem to have escaped, and wandered through Europe spreading the doctrines they had learned from the New Testament, and especially from the Epistles of St. Paul. From that time forward, in various countries of Europe, there arose individuals, or little isolated groups, who protested against the growing corruptions of the Church — and not wholly in vain, although their stories usually ended in records of martyrdom.

It must be remembered that not all at once did the professing Church depart from her pristine light and glory. There remained in her many good and holy men; and they — at least the more enlightened amongst them — stemmed, as far as they knew how, the rising tide of evil and superstition. No doubt, according to their lights, they did the main thing, helped by Christ: they taught the people to believe in Him, and to serve Him.

One of the most remarkable of these good men was Claude, Bishop of Turin, a man of great ability and of true Evangelical character, knowledge, and zeal. He lived in the ninth century, as also did our great and good King Alfred, a true follower of Jesus Christ; but Alfred lived in the second half of the century, Claude in the first. His influence, which was great, extended into countries other than his own, and especially into France. He had a great friend there, a man like-minded with himself, Agobardus, the Bishop of Lyons, who ruled a large and important diocese in Southern France.

Claude's own episcopal city, Turin, is, as you all know, the capital of Piedmont. I am sure you anticipate what I am going to say. In his diocese were the Valleys of Piedmont, where from that day to this the Protestant faith has found a refuge and a shelter. The Church of the Valleys, or the Waldensian Church, is one of the two pre-Reformation Churches which exist to this day. Its motto is *Lux lucet in tenebris* (The Light shines in darkness) — and well have its children lived up to it. Theirs is a protesting Church, but, as they themselves believe, not a reformed Church. They say that they never received the corrupt doctrines of the Church of Rome, and therefore they never cast them off. The primitive faith which they had still retained in the time of Claude, was confirmed by his teaching; and they have continued in it down to the present day — a long, unbroken record.

The constitution of their Church was primitive. At one time they had bishops; and always they have had presbyters, or pastors, carefully taught and proved, and regularly ordained by the laying on of hands. These ordinations took place in no grand cathedral, but in the heart of the mountains, in a natural fortress of rock called Pra-del-Tor. Mountains have been ever the friends of Protestantism. Often indeed have we had to say — and we love to say it,

> *For the strength of the hills we bless Thee,*
> *Our God, our fathers' God.*

From age to age, in those beautiful valleys, hemmed in by rocky mountains, the Waldenses held their faith. They were not only a witnessing Church, they were also a missionary Church. The pastors ordained amongst the rocks and the everlasting hills did not minister only to the thirteen churches in the thirteen Waldensian parishes: they went forth over all Europe. When there was darkness everywhere, these intrepid missionaries carried the light, at the peril, often at the cost, of their lives. Usually they went in the disguise of pedlars — but the wares they carried were the Word of God, the promises of Christ, and the hopes of eternal life. By their own people these pastors were called *Barbes* — the word *Barbe* meaning "Uncle," and being used as a title of respect and affection, which is still the case amongst the Negroes — a custom made familiar to us all by *Uncle Tom's Cabin*. They had books; they had the Bible in their own tongue, and they had other writings also, such as catechisms. One of their writings was called the *Nobla Leyçon* or "The Noble Lesson." It is said to date from the twelfth century, and it contains the significant words:

If there is any one who will not lie or steal,
Or commit adultery, or cheat, or sin against his neighbour,
They say he is a Vaudois, and worthy of punishment.

So, even thus early, the witnesses for truth were also the witnesses for righteousness.

In what language was the *Nobla Leyçon* written? Not Italian, nor French, nor Spanish. It was in one that has perished now, a sort of halfway house between the old Latin and the modern French and Italian. It was called the Romaunt or the Romance language. And that was the language in which the early Protestants of Piedmont and also of the South of France wrote and spoke. Rather a curious fact, is it not, when taken in connection with our subject? But it was not exactly through the Protestantism that existed amongst them that the people of Provence and of Languedoc have bequeathed to us the name of what we now call Romance. The Romaunt was their native tongue — which was sometimes called also the "Langue d'oc" — "oc" being the word for "yes" in the South of France, as "oui" was in the North — hence *Languedoc*. And Languedoc, with its adjacent provinces, was the land of the Troubadours and the Trouvères, the fathers of modern poetry, who first said and sung for modern ears the old yet ever new tales of love and war, and deeds of high enterprise, touched and heightened by the spirit of mediaeval chivalry. The land of the Troubadours was also the land of the Albigenses, that other community of early Protestants who derived their name from the town of Albi, probably because they were very numerous there, or in its neighbourhood. Our information about them is very indistinct, and, as in the case of the Paulicians, comes to us only through their enemies; but they seem to have raised the standard of protest against Rome as early as the eleventh century. They are thought to have owed much in the following century to the life and work of Peter Waldo, the merchant of

Lyons, whose statue has a place on the pedestal of the great Luther monument in Worms, as one of his forerunners. The followers of Waldo, who were known as the "Poor Men of Lyons," were active in spreading a pure and simple faith; and he gave to all who could read the Romaunt language the inestimable boon of the Bible in their own tongue — not that he translated it himself, but he induced others to do so under his patronage.

A rather amusing story is told of him, which may serve to give distinctness to the figure of a man who to most of us is little but a name. The wealthy merchant thought it his duty to take our Lord's words literally, and sell all he had to give to the poor. Before doing so, he had, very rightly, provided for the needs of his wife and children; but his own bread he begged in the streets from door to door. This greatly distressed his wife, and she complained of his conduct, with tears, to the Archbishop of Lyons. Whereupon the Archbishop sent for Waldo, and solemnly forbade him in future to ask alms from anyone except his own wife. Waldo seems to have obeyed. He had not broken with the ecclesiastical system of his time. But by and by persecution arose. Rome, with all her might, armed herself to crush the Albigenses and those who sympathized with them. In the earlier ages of the Church's history, the ages when the Goths and Vandals overthrew the Empire of Rome, and everything was left in confusion after them, the Bishops of Rome had exercised a great power for good. Almost the one stable element amidst the wreck and turmoil of the times, they had held the Church and the social order together, and helped to keep knowledge and civilization from perishing. But gradually, yet all too early, there had come a change. "That wicked servant" began to say in his heart, "My lord delayeth his coming;" he began "to beat the men-servants and the maidens, and to eat and drink with the drunken." Many of the earlier Popes had been true servants of

Christ; many of the later Popes have been — what all impartial history declares them, but what I do not care to voice. Take from poet lips a description of what they did,

> *The world-wide throes*
> *Which went to make the Popedom — the despair*
> *Of free men, good men, wise men; the dread shows*
> *Of women's faces, by the faggot's flash*
> *Tossed out, to the minutest stir and throb*
> *Of the white lips, least tremble of a lash,*
> *To glut the red stare of a licensed mob*
> *The short mad cries down oubliettes — the plash*
> *So horribly far off! priests, trained to rob;*
> *And kings that like encouraged nightmares sat*
> *On nations' hearts.*

These words describe what actually happened. The Pope ruled the priests, and the priests ruled the kings. Even in a much later and so-called enlightened age we know of a priest, the confessor of a king, who boasted: "With my God in my hand and my king at my knee, I am greater than any monarch on earth." And too often the kings, at the bidding of the priests, "like encouraged nightmares," sat upon and oppressed the people. What we read in the last Book of the Bible about the woman clothed in scarlet — an appropriate colour — sounds more like history then prophecy. She is seated on a beast, the emblem of civil or secular power, as a woman is of a Church, whether true or apostate. The rider, as you know, rules the beast at will, guiding or driving him. There came a time when the Church, acting through its head, the Pope, organized a general persecution; or — to call it what he called it himself — a Crusade, against the Albigenses, with the avowed intention of destroying them. This Pope was Innocent III, he who laid our English King John under the Interdict, and whose estimate of his office and of himself may be gathered from his own words, in which he calls himself "the lieutenant of Him who hath written upon His vesture and on His thigh, 'the King of Kings and the Lord of Lords.' I alone enjoy the plenitude of power, that others may say of me, next to God, 'And out of His fullness have we received.' "

There were two ways (amongst others), in which Innocent exercised this "plenitude of power" of which he boasted. He will be ever remembered as the father of the Inquisition, which he founded with the aid of the monk called St. Dominic — and also as the ruthless desolator of the South of France. Those countries, which before were as a garden of the Lord, favoured with every good gift of nature, well cultivated, prosperous, and inhabited by a civilized, music-loving, art-loving race, became through him almost a desert, and it was centuries before they recovered from the miseries he brought upon them.

No country perhaps, not even Holland, has been more abundantly watered with the blood of the martyrs than the South of France. You remember, in the early Pagan persecutions, the touching story of the martyrs of Lyons and Vienne. That was in the second century. And again, at the opening of the thirteenth century, another tragedy was enacted there, but on a far grander scale.

Innocent summoned a General Council of the chief men in Church and State out of all Europe, to meet at the Lateran, in Rome. He opened the Council by a sermon, taking for his text these words of our Lord, "With desire have I desired to eat this Passover with you." Oh, profane and awful blasphemy! To take these sacred words from the loving lips of our Lord, spoken just before He went forth to die for men, to consecrate a plan for the wholesale destruction of thousands of innocent men and women and children!

He proclaimed a Crusade. We have all heard of crusades against the Saracens — intended to drive them out of the Holy

Land. This one was not intended to drive men out, but to do *another thing*. The standard was raised, and that standard was the Cross — the *Cross of Christ*. Anyone who would was invited to follow it, with the promise, not only, if he fell in battle, of immediate entrance into heaven, but that if he lived, no matter what crimes he might have committed, they should all be forgiven; all his debts should be cancelled, and he should be from thenceforth a free man. You may guess the sort of army that would be gathered in that way. You may imagine the set of desperadoes, criminals, vagabonds, vagrants, who would come from all Europe to pour themselves upon the smiling, peaceful, prosperous provinces of Southern France.

The rulers of the doomed country must have had some sort of warning of the coming deluge, and have been to some extent prepared. But although there were among them several powerful barons, they had neither the strength nor the means to stand against the onset of all Europe. The barons were probably all Roman Catholics; their people were divided, partly Roman Catholics and partly Albigenses. It would seem that in some places these latter were the majority, in others not.

The greatest of the barons was Raymond, Count of Toulouse. Panic-stricken, he submitted to the Crusaders, and entreated peace, which was granted him, though on very hard, humiliating conditions. But his nephew, young Raymond Roger, Viscount of Béziers, was of another mind. "No," he said, "I will not submit; I will not give up my vassals to fire and sword and pillage. I swore to protect them as they swore to serve me, and with God's help I will keep my word." When his uncle urged him to yield, and save himself from certain ruin, he answered, "Do you think they will spare us because we are Catholics? Not they! It is our lands they want, and our goods, and we have got to fight for them. But, in any case, I will never forsake my vassals." So, gathering all the little force he had, he made a gallant stand against the great host of invaders. His chief town, Béziers, he fortified as well as he was able, and then, with some of his knights, took up his own position in the fortress of Carcassonne, where he determined to hold out to the last.

The Crusaders came against Béziers in great force, and stormed it. They asked the Abbot of Citeaux, who was with them, "How are we to know the Catholics from the 'heretics,' that we may save them alive?" "Kill them all!" was the answer, "kill them all — the Lord will know His own." So it was done; and the slaughter was frightful.

Then they came to Carcassonne; but there, finding a determined resistance, they tried to treat with Raymond Roger. "Come out to us," they said, "with all your knights and all the Catholics, and we will let you go free. But the 'heretics' we must have." "I will be flayed alive before I leave one of them to your mercy," was the answer of Raymond Roger. So brave was the defence that the Crusaders grew tired and began to murmur. The Pope's Legate sent another message to Raymond. "Come out and treat with us, you and your knights," he said this time; "you shall come and go in safety under a flag of truce." Unhappily for himself, Raymond trusted him and went. The Legate listened calmly as he pleaded with him for his people; then he said to him, "As for your people, they may do as they please; but as for your-self and your knights, you are our prisoners."[6]

So ended the brief but not inglorious career of young Raymond Roger de Béziers. He was imprisoned in his own baronial hall, but soon afterwards released by death, almost certainly the result of poison. "He wrought no deliverance on the earth" — he only tried to do it, and failed. But, as Frederick Robertson said, "Heaven is for those who have failed on earth — failed *so*."

The Crusaders took Carcassonne without difficulty; but, to their amazement, no one was found in it. There happened

---

[6] This breach of faith would have been fully approved by the Pope, whose legate he was. "To keep faith with those who have not the faith is an offence against the faith" was the maxim of Innocent III.

to be a hidden passage from the town leading to a distant place, with the secret of which some of the townsfolk were acquainted, and through which they all managed to escape. It is probable that some of them at least survived the dangers they must have encountered afterwards and made their way into other lands.

But the country was ruined. The Crusading hosts poured over it in a desolating torrent, sweeping away for ever, amongst other things, the Troubadours and Trouvères, who sang the first songs and wove the first romances of modern Europe. The Albigenses, as a people, ceased to exist. But some of them made their escape to other lands — some to Bohemia, and some to Piedmont, where they found brethren in the faith. Thus, of the two candles lit in early times one was soon extinguished. But the other burned on — and it burns on still.

Of the Waldenses of Piedmont there is so much to tell that we can only give two or three stories as samples of the whole. Through nearly all their sad yet glorious history runs the double thread of persecution and massacre, massacre and persecution, with brief, fitful gleams of repose and toleration between.

The first organized attempt at actual extermination was made upon them in the fifteenth century, and its instigator was another Pope Innocent, the eighth of the name. He also summoned a Crusade, and a mongrel army from many lands poured itself upon the valleys of Piedmont, as before upon the plains of Southern France. Things were done then which I cannot utter, and cannot bear to think of. "Man dare not tell what man dare do." In nearly all records of Romish persecution such things exist and abound. We who have to search into the records have got to read of them — and we cannot forget them. God has given us the power of remembering, but He has given us no power of *forgetting* by any act of will. We sometimes wish He had.

In this Crusade it seemed at the beginning as if the invaders would carry all before them; but the Vaudois, though habitually quiet and peaceful, were thoroughly roused to resist — and resist they did. Violence and torture and outrage turned these simple mountaineers — these Alpine shepherds and hunters — into heroes and warriors. Their weapons were swords and lances, with bows and arrows which they made for themselves, and shields covered with the skins of animals. But they had one advantage over their adversaries. Truly might it have been said,

> *It was not for their loveliness that the people*
> *blessed their God*
> *For the secret places of the hills, and the mountain*
> *heights untrod.*

In these natural fortresses they made a brave and successful stand for their homes and their lives.

Once, however, their central post on the heights of San Giovanni, near the mountains of Angrogna, seemed about to be forced. The Crusaders, having ascended the mountains by degrees, reached the natural bulwark behind which the Vaudois had placed their families. They were climbing the very rock itself — a strong, determined force led by one of their most desperate captains, and resolved, at least this time, to make an end of these obstinate "heretics." The women and children saw them come — near — nearer — even nearer still. They fell on their knees and cried aloud in agony, "O Lord, save us! O God, save us!" The enemy mocked them, and the captain, who was foremost in the climbing, drew up his visor to do so more effectively. "You shall be saved," he cried, "with a vengeance!" Then a young Vaudois drew his bow and shot. The arrow pierced the captain just where the stone struck Goliath, and he fell down the rock — dead. This dismayed the

Crusaders and gave courage to the Vaudois, who shot more arrows. A panic ensued, and the attacking party fled precipitately down the cliffs.

On another occasion, when the Vaudois were in terrible danger, there came on suddenly one of the thick mists common in that region. Or perhaps we might say without irreverence, in the words of the old Covenanter, that God "sent down a lap of His cloak to screen" His persecuted people. It did not trouble *them*, for they knew every inch of the ground; but to their foes it was death. In the rocky paths and down the cliffs they stumbled and fell, while the Vaudois shot them with their arrows. So completely were they destroyed that of the whole band only one man was left alive; he was the standard-bearer. He hid in a ravine and stayed there two days. Then he said to himself, "I may as well be killed by the 'heretics' as die here of starvation and misery." So he came out of his hiding-place. But, to his amazement, the "heretics" did *not* kill him. They gave him food and shelter, and then sent him home to his own country. It was he who told the story of the fate of his comrades.

After the Crusade in which these things happened, though the Vaudois were continually exposed to persecution, there does not seem to have been for a considerable time any fresh attempt to destroy them utterly in their native valleys.

Many were the martyrs who suffered; we shall take from the crowded records, almost at random, the story of one as a sample of the rest; because we usually realize better and feel more the doings and the sufferings of one man than of many. Geoffrey Varaille, pastor of the Waldensian Church, was not a Waldensian by birth. On the contrary, he was the son of one of the ferocious military leaders who had taken part in the horrible Crusade against them. He was a clever boy, so he gave himself to study and in due time became a priest. He took up his residence at a town in Piedmont, near the valleys. He would have liked to convert the "heretic" people there — but rather, it would seem, by argument and persuasion than by the methods his father had adopted. He became well known for his zeal, his eloquence, and his learning, and by and by was invited by his superiors to go on a preaching tour in Italy. Here his fame increased, and bright prospects opened before him. But he did not forget the poor lost "heretics," whom he longed to bring back to the fold of the Church.

With twelve like-minded companions whom he gathered about him, he began an earnest and, no doubt, prayerful study of the difference between the two religions. This led to questions, which his companions seem to have shared; and they came, after a time, under suspicion of heresy themselves. For four or five years they were all imprisoned, but at the end of that time Varaille was released — we know not how or why. Still undecided in mind, he went with the Papal Legate to Paris. There he heard of the cruel massacre of the Vaudois colonists who had settled in the French districts of Merindol and Cabrières, and of whom Louis XII, King of France, said after candid inquiry, "They are better Christians than we are." This apparently was the deciding point of his life.

But by that time the lamp kept burning so bravely in the valleys of Piedmont was no longer the sole Evangelical light.

In God's ripe fields the day [was] cried —

the Reformation was in full progress. Varaille went to Geneva to confer with Calvin, and came back to Piedmont to be ordained in the Pra-del-Tor as a humble pastor of the Waldensian Church. He was now nearly fifty, but the faith — which, though old as the ages, is yet ever young — made him young again. He preached and taught with all diligence, his knowledge of Italian proving very useful. At last, on a visit to his birthplace, he was apprehended. At first he was kindly treated, on account of the reverence felt for his character and his abilities. He might have escaped, but refused to do so, having given his parole. But eventually he was sent in chains to Turin, where he was tried, and condemned to be burned. When his sentence was pronounced he said to his judges: "Be assured, my lords, you will sooner want wood wherewith to burn us than men ready to burn in seal of their faith. From day to day they multiply, and the 'Word of God endureth for ever'." That was the last word of Geoffrey Varaille to the Church and to the world. He died without suffering, having been — through the humanity, it is said, of the executioner — strangled at the stake.

One more story of the Waldenses must be told. It is of what is called in history "*La Glorieuse Rentrée*," the "Glorious Return" to their Alpine homes. But we have first to tell how and why they came to leave them.

Of their own accord we may be sure they never would have left them. They would rather have died there, reddening the soil with their blood, as generation after generation had done before, for "the Word of God and for the testimony of Jesus Christ."

Persecution and massacre — massacre and persecution — so from century to century the tale went on. The seventeenth century was worse perhaps than any that had preceded it. We Englishmen and Englishwomen remember with pride and satisfaction the noble interference of Cromwell on behalf of the oppressed, and the immortal words of his poet-secretary, John Milton,

Avenge, O Lord, Thy slaughtered saints, whose bones
Lie scatter'd on the Alpine mountains old;
Ev'n them who kept Thy truth so pure of old,
When all our fathers worshipp'd stocks and stones,
Forget not: in Thy book record their groans

Who were Thy sheep, and in their ancient fold
Slain by the bloody Piedmontese that roll'd
Mother with infant down the rocks. Their moans
The vales redoubled to the hills and they
To Heaven. Their martyred blood and ashes sow
O'er all the Italian fields, where still doth sway
The triple tyrant; that from these may grow
A hundredfold, who having learned the way,
Early may fly the Babylonian woe.

Some thirty years later a yet worse storm swept over the valleys. Then it was that those who escaped death by the sword — or by other more horrible means — were driven from their mountain homes, which were left to ruin and desolation. There were no longer any Waldensians in the Waldensian valleys. The rightful owners; forbidden to return on pain of death, found refuge as they could in foreign countries. But the Powers which had carried out this horrible policy of murder and expatriation did not want these rich and fertile valleys to be deserted, so they tried to colonize them. Once and again they tried, but without success. Colonists of the right sort would not come, or would not stay; and colonists of the wrong sort did more harm than good. At last they put up the valleys to auction; but neither did this plan prove a success. For the most part they lay deserted — vineyards ruined, fields overgrown with weeds, houses crumbling away.

There was amongst the exiles a Huguenot pastor, who, driven from Dauphiné by persecution, had pursued his calling amongst the Waldenses of Piedmont until forced to share their exile. Henri Arnaud mourned and pondered over the desolation of the valleys he loved, until there came to him the thought that their rightful inhabitants might get them back again. Surely they ought to try, and God would help them to do it! He, for one, was ready to risk his life in the attempt. Almost every one tried to persuade him against it. "What could a homeless fugitive — or a handful of such fugitives — quite unused to war, do against the united forces of France and Savoy? It was a dream. It was impossible."

But "faith laughs at impossibilities." With faith like that of Gideon, Henri Arnaud gathered a little band of eight hundred men, most of them exiles from the valleys, the rest Huguenots, like himself. They assembled by night in Geneva, went down to a quiet place on the lake, and took possession of some fishermen's boats, probably left there for the purpose. They sailed across the lake to the territory of Savoy. Here the inhabitants were bitterly hostile, and French and Savoyard forces were ready to oppose them at every turn. One regular battle was fought. The Vaudois had to pass through a narrow defile, and then by a bridge over the little river Dore. A Savoyard army behind opened upon them a destructive fire, while a strong French force before them held the bridge. Arnaud bade them lie down on their faces to escape the fire, while he, with three brave companions, held in check a band that tried to charge them in the rear. Still, they were in the jaws of death: they could neither advance nor retreat.

Suddenly a voice cried out, "Courage, the bridge is ours!" At the word the brave eight hundred sprang to their feet, rushed forward with resistless impetuosity, and carried all before them. The bridge *was* won. What a lesson for us! Assume that the thing that should be done *is* done, and we get the strength to do it.

Then they marched on to their beloved valleys, with thoughts that have been well voiced for them in the patriot song,

Our feet again shall stand
Where our valiant fathers trod;
And we'll send this shout o'er our native land,
"For our country and our God!"

Eight months of conflict with vastly superior forces still lay before them — and would there were room to tell the story of it here! But at the end they triumphed. They occupied their ancient homes again, and their descendants occupy them still.

And there may God keep them — and keep them pure and faithful witnesses for Christ and for His Truth until He comes! — UNTIL HE COMES.

* * *

But as we are talking of the long story of the ages we must needs ask, "In what age of the world did these things occur?" The date of the *Glorieuse Rentrée* was 1689, close upon the beginning of the eighteenth century. Just fourteen years before, the immortal dreamer of the *Pilgrim's Progress* saw amongst his visions "a cave where two giants, Pope and Pagan, dwelt long ago." "Pagan," he says, "has been dead many a day, while as for the other, though he be yet alive . . . he can now do little more than sit in his cave's mouth, grinning at pilgrims as they go by, and biting his nails because he cannot come at them." How little he knew of what was going on even then, and of what was yet to be done at the instigation of this same giant Pope! Even while he wrote, the Waldenses of Piedmont were undergoing cruelties surpassing those which Faithful had to suffer in Vanity Fair. And also, at that very time, there was being planned and prepared one of the most horrible persecutions the world has ever seen. Well has Miss Betham Edwards, an accomplished student of history, called the Revocation Terror "the worst terror of French or other history." The same man by whose fiat — under the influence of Rome and the Jesuits — this Terror was ordained, was also the instigator of the Piedmont massacres and tortures. And yet Louis XIV is styled in history Louis the Great, Louis the Magnificent. He bequeathed his heart to the Jesuits — and we wish them joy of it!

The formal Revocation of the Edict of Nantes took place in 1685, but the persecution had really begun some time before that, and it lasted — do you know how long? The law condemning Protestant pastors to death for the mere exercise of their office remained on the Statute Book of France until a very few years before the Revolution. Nor was it long since the spirit of the age had succeeded in making it a dead letter. We mentioned already one of these martyred pastors, named Majal Désubas. A friend well known to some of us, a sister of the distinguished President of Westfield College, during a recent visit to France actually saw and spoke with the grand-niece of Désubas. Nor was he the last to vindicate on a scaffold and in the face of the world the right of Protestants to their name in its Greek form. The father of the present Bishop of Durham, in the year 1850, dined with an aged lady, brought over to England, when very young, by her father, to escape the persecution in France. She must have been twelve years old when François Rochette, the last of the long and glorious line of martyred pastors, died on the scaffold.

Though he was the last to suffer death in this cause "in the face of the sun and the eye of day" we have reason to think he was by no means the last who was killed, or done to death, through the machinations of Rome — as for instance in Italy, under the hateful rule of King Bomba.[7]

There are many people, we believe, who think the martyrs of the Reformation and the martyrs of Protestantism quite synonymous expressions. We hope our slight and most imperfect sketch may give them some faint idea, of the multitude that came before and the multitude that followed after that great epoch in the Church's history.

---

[7] Numberless instances of Roman Catholic intolerance and persecution, within living memory and even in our own day, could be given by those acquainted with the subject. In Ireland, for instance, such stories abound, and they are sometimes very touching and pathetic. But they do not fall within our province.

THE ROMANCE OF VICTORY

(THE STORY OF HOLLAND)

Freedom's battle, once begun,
Bequeathed from bleeding sire to son,
Though baffled oft, is ever won.
                    — SIR WALTER SCOTT

From *William of Orange: the Silent Prince*
by W.G. Van de Hulst

V

THE ROMANCE OF VICTORY

(THE STORY OF HOLLAND)

Amongst the things for which Protestantism witnesses, we have named, and we have every right to name — *Freedom*.

It is not the greatest thing, but it is a great thing, for all that, we have ventured to say that no one who has studied history, with anything like impartiality, can deny the services that Protestantism has rendered to the cause of freedom. These are shown in the history of many countries; one will serve as an example — the story of one of the smallest countries of Europe. This country was not, like the home of the Waldenses, a land of mountains and valleys, where the hunted people could take refuge in their natural caves and fortresses with the song on their lips,

> *For the strength of the hills we bless Thee,*
> *Our God, our father's God.*

In this land there are no mountains, scarce even any hills. It lies low, flat, level with the sea, from which indeed a good part of it has been rescued by the energy, the skill, and the determination of its inhabitants. Those inhabitants showed early that they had in them the qualities of men, and of brave, strong men. And that little nation, which fought the sea for generations for the possession of that little land, in the sixteenth century fought with Spain, then the greatest of the nations, for a nobler possession — and won it.

Look at Spain on the map, and then look at Holland. The difference in size will strike you at once; but it will give you no idea at all of the difference in power between the two in the days when Holland fought with Spain. For the Spain of the sixteenth century was not the Spain of the twentieth. She was then the greatest Power in Europe; most people would have foretold that the future was with her, and that she was destined for the foremost and grandest place in the modern world.

Spain then seemed the Lucifer of nations, the child of the morning. Her monarch, in whose reign the great drama of the Netherlands began, was also the Emperor of Germany, that Charles V who presided at the Diet of Worms, who conquered his rival, Francis I, and who crushed the Schmalkaldic League. He was regarded in that age as the successor of the old emperors of Rome. His son, Philip II, who succeeded him as King of Spain though not as Emperor of Germany, succeeded also to his hereditary dominions, which comprised the Netherlands. Philip had one immense advantage, added to all his other sources of wealth and power. The treasures of the New World were at his feet. Peru and Mexico yielded up to him and his their untold riches in gold and silver. No empty vaunt was the answer of the Spanish Ambassador to those who boasted to him of the vast resources of France, "*My master's treasury has no bottom.*"

Yet the men in that little corner of Europe which we call Holland, fought with Philip and conquered him, and tore their freedom from his reluctant hands. Now if a nation wants to be free there are three things which it ought to have, and which if it has will almost certainly secure its freedom. These three things are: Some men who can die; many men who can fight; one man who can rule. Holland had them all. We will take them in order.

1. Some men who can die. These are the kind of men Protestantism has always made wherever it has found entrance.

You remember the saying, "He who can die cannot be compelled," and wherever there are men who cannot be compelled, there are sown the ineradicable seeds of freedom.

Into the Netherlands, which included what we now call Holland, and Belgium also, the Protestant Faith found early entrance. The proto-martyrs of the Reformation were from the Low Countries, and from that beginning, in 1523, the blood of martyrs never ceased to flow. No part of Europe, probably, had so many martyrs, except France. The author of the *Chronicles of the Schönberg-Cotta Family* has put this in a striking way. "Anyone who is in search of relics may take up any handful from the earth of Holland, and be pretty sure it contains the dust of a martyr." We may call these martyrs indeed not merely numerous, but innumerable. In old, half-forgotten records we find a crowd of names, but often the names are all we find, and oftener still the very names even are not recorded. It may be said of them, as of the heroes who lived before Homer, "They had no bard, and died." No one sang their praises no one told the tale of their sufferings and their glory. But these things are recorded elsewhere — as we know.

The "Edicts" under which they suffered emanated first from the Emperor Charles, and were confirmed and strengthened by his bigoted and fanatical son, Philip II. If there is any name in history worthy of the execration of humanity it is certainly that of Philip II. These edicts against heresy were just as severe as the laws of the Spanish Inquisition. The free-hearted men of Holland complained continually that Spain was imposing the Inquisition upon them. The King of Spain used to answer, "No, it is not the Inquisition;" meaning it was not the Spanish Inquisition — but in fact it *was* the Inquisition all the same. In some respects it was even worse, if worse could be. In order to be burned at the stake a man had not to profess the doctrines of Luther or Calvin, he had only to read a few chapters of the Bible in his own house and to his own family; he had only to have in his possession a book of Luther's, even if he had got it out of mere curiosity; he had only to abstain from going to Mass; he had only to utter a few words of compassion for the "heretics" he saw on their way to the fire, to involve himself in the same terrible doom. Just to give distinctness to our thoughts of this great army of victims we will give one or two personal touches.

One man, a schoolmaster, was brought before a particularly zealous inquisitor named Titelman. He prayed to have his case transferred to the civil tribunal, but the inquisitor said, "No, you are my prisoner, and to me, and me alone, you must answer. You have a wife and children; have you no pity for them? Do you not love them?"

"Love my wife and children!" said the martyr. "God knows that if the world were gold, and I had the whole of it, I would give it all, only to be with them, even if it were on bread and water and in banishment."

"You have them," returned the inquisitor, "if you will only renounce your errors."

"Neither for wife nor children, nor for the whole world, will I renounce my God and His truth," was the answer.

He was sent to the stake.

Sometimes whole families incurred this doom. A man named Robert Ogier, with his wife and two sons, was brought before the judges on the charge that none of them went to Mass, but read the Bible, and prayed by themselves in their own house. They confessed the offence, and were asked what rites they practiced at home. One of the sons, who was only a boy, answered with boyish simplicity, "We kneel down and pray to God; we ask Him to enlighten our hearts and to forgive us our sins. Also we pray for our king, and for the magistrates, and for all in authority, that God may protect and preserve them." The judges were softened; some of them even shed tears. But all the same, both father and son were condemned to the stake. When they came to the place of execution the boy prayed, "Eternal Father, accept the sacrifice of our lives in the name of Thy beloved Son!" And as the flames rose about them, he cried aloud to his father, "Look, my father, all heaven is opening, and I see ten hundred thousand angels rejoicing over us. Let us be glad, for we are dying for the truth." Eight days later, the mother and the younger son were brought out and burned. "So," adds the chronicler, "there was an end of that family."

On another occasion a man named John de Swarte, and his wife and four children, were surprised in their own house, reading the Bible and praying. There were with them two newly married couples and two other persons. All the twelve were dragged before the judgment-seat, condemned, and burned in one fire.

The story of Dirk Willemzoon deserves mention, if only from its connection with that kind of "romance" which will ever consecrate the "generous deed." Dirk was a Protestant escaping from his pursuers in the depths of winter over a frozen lake. The pursuers were close behind him when the ice broke, and the officer of justice, who was foremost amongst them, fell into the water. The hunted man, hearing his cry, turned back, dragged him out, and placed him in safety. By that time, however, the others had come up. In spite of some faint remonstrance from the man he had saved, Dirk Willemzoon was apprehended, brought back, and condemned. His death was one of unusually terrible and lingering agony. This was the reward man gave him for his act of self-forgetting heroism. Happily, he went to another place where, we may assume, his reward was different.

2. What we need to realize is the great number of these martyrs. The men in the Low Countries who could die were not only "some," but many — very many. But although it is

true that "the blood of the martyrs is the seed of the Church," it is quite as truly the test of the nation. We think it will be found that as the nations have dealt with God's witnesses, so God has dealt with them — so they have prospered, or not prospered, afterwards. In some countries the heart of the nation approved the death of the martyrs; they regarded it with solemn satisfaction, as a most right and acceptable sacrifice to God — as in Spain. Or — what was worse — they beheld it with savage joy, counting it a delightful entertainment — as too often in France. But in other countries the heart of the nation was touched — was revolted. It rose up and said to the rulers, "Stop this thing. We will not have it! You *must* stop it, or we'll make you." It was so in Scotland, where men said of the first Reformation martyr, Patrick Hamilton, that "the reek of his burning did infect every spot that it blew upon." It was so in England also, though it took a longer time and more martyrs to do it. It was so in Holland and the adjacent Provinces. It took a long time to rouse them — but roused they were at last.

Then came the Beggars' League, with the famous wallet and bowl for its badge and its symbol. The whole dramatic story — does it not live for ever in the brilliant pages of Motley's *Rise of the Dutch Republic*? Then came, in various places, tumultuous risings of the people and efforts to rescue the victims. Then came the fury of the Iconoclasts — the image-breaker — who wrecked cathedrals and churches, and destroyed sacred images and pictures. Not that this was the work of the Reformed, as a body; it was only that of a few fanatics, maddened by persecution and joined by the rabble of the great cities, intent upon satisfying their malice or their greed. And at the worst — their enemies themselves being witnesses — "they took good care not to injure in any way the living images." But all these things showed that it was time for the many men who could fight to take the matter in hand — and they did.

When resistance to tyranny began, at first measures were taken to put it down by force, and the prospects of the patriots looked dark, very dark indeed. In the year 1568 a thing was done in Spain by the tribunal of the Inquisition which in these days can hardly be believed. What do you think was the greatest death sentence ever pronounced in the world? I have no doubt it was this one. The Inquisition actually doomed to death the whole population of the country — men, women, and children — numbering three million. Three million people doomed to death in three lines! Only a few exceptions were made, *by name*. Ten days later Philip confirmed by his royal authority this stupendous Death Sentence. And to show that it was no mere bravado, no threat to frighten the rebellious into submission, he sent an army, presumably to execute it. This army was under the command of the ferocious Duke of Alva, whose name is familiar to us all. For five terrible years his iron grip was on the nation's throat, and the history of these years is "written within and without with mourning and lamentation and woe." Truly indeed was "the earth like a winepress trod." Horrible as had been the atrocities of the preceding years, these five outdid them all.

It was a carnival of violence, injustice, and cruelty. But it came to an end, and that soon — because God gave to the nation, not only some men who could die and many men who could fight, but the third requisite for achieving freedom — one man who could rule.

3. Will you, for a little while, turn back your thoughts some fifteen years, to the striking and dramatic scene in the great Hall of Brussels, where the Emperor Charles V, of his own free will, is laying down the heavy burden of his double sovereignty? There he stands, before that splendid and most illustrious assembly, an old and broken man — though his years were but fifty-five — to speak his words of farewell, and make his solemn Act of Abdication. On his right stands

his son, Philip, the heir of his Spanish dominions — yet looking anything but like a Spaniard, for he is of fair complexion, and equally unlike a king, for he is undersized, mean-faced, without distinction of bearing, and with the repulsive hanging under-lip and prominent jaw which characterized his race. On the left of the Emperor stands a young man of twenty-two, on whose arm he is leaning. Tall, splendidly handsome, of noble bearing, dark-complexioned like a Spaniard and magnificently attired, you might have thought him more fit than Philip to be the king of Spain.

Very different, however, was to be the destiny of William of Nassau, Prince of Orange. But just then he knew not of it. Life was opening out its fairest prospects before him. Rich, gifted, brilliant, ambitious, he already enjoyed the special favour of the Emperor, whose page he had been from his childhood. Charles, an excellent judge of character, used to allow him, when only fifteen, to be present, as his personal attendant, at his most secret Councils, because he knew that, even then, he was utterly to be trusted. Even then he knew how to keep silence — a quality which won for him in after years the name of William the Silent — not that he was silent in conversation; on the contrary, he was said to be particularly bright, ready, and genial. In his youth he threw himself heartily into the pursuits of ambition and into the pleasures of his age, and seemed bent on enjoying life to the uttermost. But He whom he knew not then, knew him, and had other work prepared for him.

A few years after the Emperor's abdication, when peace was made between France and Spain, William was sent to France as one of the hostages, the other being the terrible Duke of Alva. During his stay, the King of France, Henry II, was concocting with his former enemy, Philip of Spain, a secret plot for the destruction of the Protestants of both countries. As said before, this meant nothing short of their absolute and utter extermination. Alva was in the secret but, for sufficient reasons, it had not been entrusted to William of Orange.

One day Henry was riding at the Chase in the Forest of Vinçennes, and finding himself alone with William, began to talk to him about the plot, not knowing, or forgetting, his ignorance of it. What he heard struck home with a great horror to the young man's heart. He was no Protestant, he was a Roman Catholic, like all those around him; but, as he himself said afterwards, "the thought of so many innocent and virtuous people being put to death struck into my heart with a sense of horror." So prudent was he, however, that he not only held his peace at the time, allowing Henry fully to unfold his plan, but did not for long afterwards mention it to anyone. It is said to have been this incident which especially procured him the name of William the Silent. It did more; it seems to have awakened in his strong and generous heart a steadfast determination to help and save the persecuted Protestants, wherever he could, and especially in the Provinces of Holland, Zeeland, and Utrecht, of which he was hereditary Stadtholder. Holland was the largest and most powerful of these, and therefore it has given its name not only to the three, but (unofficially) to the seven which, under his auspices, succeeded in gaining their independence, and which now compose the kingdom of the Netherlands.

On the coming of Alva, William left the country, or he would most certainly never have lived to do anything more for it. His friends, Egmont and Horn, in spite of his earnest entreaties, chose to stay, confident in their innocence, and both died on the scaffold.

But he went to come back again. He gathered in Germany a little army of volunteers, and with this he came to the help of the brave people who had already begun the fight for faith and freedom. Already the "Sea Beggars," as they were called — the wild sea rovers, half pirates, half patriots, who were an outcome and offshoot of the famous Beggars' League — had taken the seaport of Brill, and towns here and there were rising against the Spaniards. Still, the enterprise was desperate. While his expedition was preparing, friends in Germany asked him, "But what alliances have you? Which of the kings or princes will take your part? How do you intend to keep up this war?"

William's answer showed that great thoughts had been at work within him. Much was changed there, since the Emperor leaned on his arm in Brussels, and even since King Henry talked with him in the Forest of Vinçennes. "Before I ever took up the cause of the oppressed Christians in these Provinces," he said, "I had entered into a close alliance with the King of kings, and I am firmly convinced that all who put their trust in Him shall be saved by His Almighty hand." True; but those who trust Him have to wait for His salvation — and sometimes, as it seems to us, to wait long for it. Twice was his little army discomfited, and he himself driven out of the country by the overwhelming Spanish forces. But he came again the third time — and this time he came to stay. When asked what he would do if conquered, he said, "I will die in the last ditch."[8]

The story of the long and desperate war that followed abounds in thrilling scenes and incidents, and will amply repay an attentive perusal. We cannot give it here; we can only take one episode as a sample of the rest — the siege of Leyden. The town is about fifteen miles from the sea-coast; and those miles have been mostly rescued from the waters by the courage and industry of the inhabitants. The sea is kept back by a wonderful and cunning arrangement of dykes and barriers; and at the time of the war those fifteen miles were a smiling

---

[8] The author is confusing two Williams of Orange here. It was William III of Orange — who later led the Glorious Revolution and became king of England — who spoke these words when the French armies had invaded the major part of the Netherlands in 1672. — Editor.

country, well watered, full of cereal crops and other good fruits of the earth. Leyden had already undergone a short and ineffectual siege, which was raised by means of Count Louis of Nassau, the brother of William, who had come from France to help the good cause. The Spaniards had to abandon the siege and march to oppose him, so for that time the town was delivered. William had four brothers, all true friends of Holland and of Protestantism. Three of them died in battle, only one was left with him to the end, to be his trusted friend and counsellor. They had a good mother, Juliana of Stolberg, still living at this time, a truly Christian woman, who helped them by her counsel and her prayers.

It was in March, 1574, that the first siege of Leyden was raised. But in May, after the defeat and death of Louis of Nassau, the Spaniards came back in great force, and the town was besieged again. Unhappily, the people thought, when the first danger had passed, that they were quite safe and all would go well. So they neglected to lay in a sufficient stock of provisions, and the Spaniards took them unprepared. Still, it was of the utmost importance that they should hold out to the last, for the sake of the whole country, to which Leyden might be called the key, and also for their own. For whenever the Spaniards took a town they committed the most horrible cruelties upon the defenceless inhabitants. Haarlem, for instance, after a brilliant resistance in which women and children fought on the ramparts beside the men, capitulated on the solemn promise that all lives should be spared, which promise the Spaniards broke with horrible treachery, putting to death 2,300 persons in cold blood. That was a good warning, not for Leyden alone, but for the whole country.

It was on the 26th of May that the siege began. The citizens had sent word to William, "We will hold out for one month with bread, and for another month without bread." In fact, they had only bread for one month in the city, and that was by reducing every one's allowance — each citizen got only half a pound a day, at the end of the first month the bread was gone, and for another month they made shift with malt-cake. Still no prospect of relief. They were able, by means of carrier pigeons, to hold occasional communication with their friends outside, to tell them their condition, and receive messages from them. William, with his small, inadequate army, was burning to deliver them; but what could he do? At last, from toil and sorrow and anxiety, he fell into a fever, and was "nigh unto death." Still he kept on counseling and encouraging the men of Leyden, and trying to help them. He took care that they should not know of his illness, which would almost have driven them to despair. Under his directions the Dutch Admiral, Boisot, collected a fleet and brought it to the sea-coast, fifteen miles away. But there it had to stay, for ships do not sail over land. Then William came to the heroic resolution that he would have all the dykes cut, that the sea might overflow the land and bring the ships to the city. Of course this involved the destruction of the crops, the fruits — everything that grew upon the ground — in fact, the ruin of the whole district. But William said, "Better a drowned land than a lost land," and so, with the consent of the owners of the property, the dykes were cut. But this was a serious business, and a long one. So ingenious and so complicated was the system contrived to keep the waters out, that it was by no means easy to let them in, even when people wanted to do it.

And now that there was no more bread, no more malt-cake even, what were the men of Leyden to do? They began to eat any sort of thing they could lay their hands upon. The leaves were soon stripped from all the trees that grew in the town. And, as their need increased, far worse things came to be eaten — things horrible and revolting. A small number of cows had been kept for the sick and the infants, and a few of these were slaughtered every day, and their flesh distributed in the smallest morsels. Every drop of blood was used, and the very skins were boiled and eaten. Like shadows of their former selves, the miserable inhabitants stole about the streets. Sometimes they fell down dead as they walked. Children died like flies, and old people too. Delicate ladies used to go and search the dung-heaps, in the hope of finding some edible morsel there. Dogs and cats, rats and mice were esteemed rare luxuries.

Meanwhile the besiegers, knowing what the besieged must be suffering, and beginning to see how hard they were to conquer, tried to tempt them to surrender. They would spare their lives; they would treat them very gently; they would give them favourable terms — if only they would yield the city. The answer was this: "You call us eaters of dogs and cats. Very well. So long, then, as in this city you hear a dog bark or a cat mew, you may know we will not yield. And when all else is done, we will eat our left arms and keep our right to fight for our Country, our Faith, and our God. At last, if we have to die, we will set fire to the city and perish in the flames."

These indeed were men who could die; and the women were brave also, sometimes even braver than the men.

All this time there was the fleet lying in the offing, the dykes were cut, the land submerged and ruined, but still the waters would not rise enough to float the ships. The men of Leyden, in their misery, used to climb to the top of the high tower of St. Pancras, from where they could see the ships all laden with food, while they were starving and their anguish passing slowly into utter despair. We cannot suppose that every one in the city had the spirit of a hero or a martyr; so we need not wonder that some of the citizens, half mad with hunger, and seeing their dear ones suffer with them, said in their hearts, "What use in resisting any more? The Spaniards must have us in the end. And better first than last. Death will come the quicker." But the burgomaster, Van der Werf, was a true hero.

With the help of Van der Does, the like-minded commandant, he had directed the defence and kept order in the city, bravely sustaining all the time the courage of the people. But at last a tumult arose. An angry crowd gathered round him in the market-place, and cried aloud — in the rage that was half despair — "We can bear it no longer. You must yield — you must yield — or we will make you! We are starving!"

Van der Werf took off his broad-brimmed hat and waved it, to ask for silence. Then he said, "Citizens and brothers, I would feed you, but I cannot. I am as hungry as you. But this I know and say: I have sworn to God that I would keep this city — and keep it I will. I will not surrender. I care nothing for my own life. Kill me; tear my flesh in pieces, and let the most hungry among you devour it! But yield this city I will not."

The people, moved to the heart, vowed that they would stand by him to the last — and they did. Worse and worse the suffering grew. At this time, unhappily, the wind was easterly, so it blew the waters away from the land instead of upon it; and the despairing citizens, looking from the tower of St. Pancras, could only fix their glazing eyes on the distant ships, and think they were going to die of hunger with help and plenty in their very sight.

There was a strong dyke within five miles of the city, called the Landscheiding. With a great effort the soldiers of freedom outside had gotten possession of this, and cut it. But still the waters would not rise, and still the foe was beneath the walls. And moreover, the Spaniards had erected forts close to the city — especially one strong one, called the Lammen fort — from which, even if the waters should rise, it would be very difficult to dislodge them. On every side hope seemed cut off.

It came to the night of the first of October. That night the wind changed. The despairing people thanked God when they had climbed to St. Pancras tower, and, weak with hunger as they were, found it hard to stand against the freshening breeze that was now blowing *from the west*. It grew and strengthened until it became a gale, bearing toward them the waters — the welcome waters, the blessed waters, the waters of deliverance — upon which was the fleet, laden with the food they were dying for! Oh, but there would still be that fort, right in the way of the deliverers — how were they to pass it?

The second day came, and the second night. During that night a tremendous noise was heard, which intensified the alarm and horror of the citizens, who, in the thick darkness, could not tell what had happened. But at daybreak a boy came to the burgomaster and said, "Sir, I want to tell you I was standing on the rampart, and as I looked toward the Lammen fort I saw many lights — a long line of lights — and they were moving *away from it*. Sir, I think the Spaniards are gone."

"That cannot be," said Van der Werf. "They would never abandon their most important fort like that. It is impossible."

"But I am sure of it, Sir," the boy persisted. "If you give me leave I will go out and see."

"No," was the answer, "you must not go, for you would certainly be killed. It would be throwing your life away."

"I must die anyway," the boy returned, "for I am starving. Oh, Sir, I pray of you, let me go!" The burgomaster let him go. By and by the watchers on the rampart saw a boy standing at the top of the Lammen fort and wildly waving his cap. It was quite true. The fort was abandoned. The mysterious noise in the night — which was really caused by the fall of a part of the city wall — had created a panic in the garrison, already alarmed by the rising of the waters, and they thought it better not to wait to be drowned. A man, wading breast-high through the water, bore the joyful news to the fleet, which had now begun to move. The last obstacle to its coming was no more.

In the abandoned fort the boy found a pot filled with vegetables — carrots, turnips, and onions — which some Spanish soldier had prepared for a late supper or an early breakfast. He took up the pot, and carried it into the town; and that was the first food that came into Leyden after the siege. That pot is still preserved in the Leyden Museum.

The people, now full of hope, crowded down to the quay. And there, when the sun arose, a sight yet more glorious met their view — the ships of their deliverers moving upon the waters, those blessed waters! What words can tell the rapture of that sight! Even before the ships touched the quay the men in them threw out food — bread and herrings — to the starving people. When they reached it, the first to land was Admiral Boisot. The heroic burgomaster, Van der Werf, stood on the quay awaiting him, and the two — the admiral an old, white-haired man, the burgomaster not old, but worn with toil and care and suffering — fell into each other's arms, and wept and sobbed aloud. So did those around them. Yet the first thing the people thought of was to give thanks to God. Deliverers and delivered together, they streamed with one impulse to the largest church in the town, the church of St. Peter. The pastor offered a thanksgiving prayer — then the mass of voices rose in song — probably in Luther's immortal hymn, the Marseillaise of the Reformation,

Our God is our strong Hiding-place,
Our sole Defence and Tower;
He helps us freely by His Grace
In every evil hour.

The hymn was never finished, the whole multitude broke down and wept together like children. But no doubt He to whom they turned in joy, as they had done in sorrow, "Discerned, in speechless fears, both prayer and praise."

That was the 3rd of October, 1574; and to the present time that day is kept in Leyden as a festival and a holiday. Every one makes it a point to partake of a dish of carrots and other vegetables in memory of the first food brought into the town after the siege. And, what is more important, every one goes to church and thanks God for His mercies. It is good for us all to say, "O God, we have heard with our ears, and our fathers have declared unto us, the noble works that Thou didst in their days, and in the old time before them."

The resistance of Leyden, and other events of the war which showed the same indomitable spirit, seem to have convinced Philip of Spain that it would not be very easy to execute his famous Death Sentence, and that after all it might be expedient rather to make terms with the delinquents. Accordingly, he published an Amnesty, in which he graciously promised to forgive all their sins and all their transgressions; and that upon the sole condition that they should return to the fold of the Catholic Church. He told them how often he had longed to gather them under his protection, "as a hen does gather her chickens under her wings." One may just remark in passing that if Philip II was a hen, he was certainly the most bloodthirsty fowl that has ever been heard of since the world began! The Amnesty proved a complete failure. The patriots treated it with contempt. Not for anything he could promise, or threaten, would they violate their consciences or forsake their religion.

Still, after the deliverance of Leyden, dark days came again, and their faith was long and sorely tried. William of Orange stood by them and upheld them through all. He had now openly joined the Reformed Communion, to which thenceforth he adhered with heart and soul. He had become, what in his youth he certainly was not, a deeply religious man.

But even he, though he knew and felt that he and his would never yield, sometimes came to fear that they must die.

Remember that now the only insuperable difference between them and Philip was that of religion; if they would become Roman Catholics all else would be conceded. But if not — Ah, do you remember another "But if not," in that wonderful story in the Book of Daniel? The answer of William of Orange and the men of Holland to the King of Spain was almost as heroic as that of Shadrach, Meshach, and Abednego to the King of Babylon: "Rather than forsake our Faith we will open all the dykes in our country — the dykes our forefathers spent their lives in making — we will give our whole land back to the sea it was taken from. And we ourselves, with our women and children, will crowd into every ship we can find, and go away into the New World, there to seek a place where we can worship God in peace and freedom." Did ever a nation come to a braver resolve than that? But they were not put to the test. God gave them their country — and their freedom too.

How in the end they won it must be read elsewhere. The little space that remains to us here must be given to the one man who, because he could rule, enabled the many men who could fight to gain the victory. Philip who could not conquer him, put him "under the Ban" — outlawed him in fact, though he was a sovereign prince like himself. He did more — he set a price upon his head. In this Ban, which was published everywhere, he promised that anyone who should take the life of William of Nassau should receive as a reward the sum of twenty-five thousand crowns in gold. "And," adds the King, "if he has committed any crime, however heinous, we promise to pardon him; and if he be not already noble, we will ennoble him for his valour." This was nothing less than a call to all the rascality of his dominions, and indeed of all Europe, to arm itself against the life of a single man, with a king's ransom for the assassin's reward. Philip's own General and relative, the Prince of Parma, remarked very meaningly, "I fear the world will say of us, that when we were unable to conquer the Prince of Orange we arranged to have him assassinated."

Two attempts were made upon the life of the Prince. The first time he was shot through the head; but, after a long and dangerous illness and much suffering, he recovered.

There is one thing about this matter which is worth recording, as it throws light upon the character of William, and upon something else also. Tremendous issues, in those days, hung upon the lives of kings and princes, so it is no wonder these were continually aimed at, and that the hands of a host of fanatics and desperadoes were armed against them. They must have lived in perpetual fear of assassination; which could not have been very pleasant, as life was at least as dear to them as to other people. Most of them took all the precautions they could; and who could blame them?

One of these precautions was to make things very unpleasant — very remarkably unpleasant indeed — for their would-be assassins, when they succeeded in catching them. The accounts of the punishments inflicted upon those who murdered, or tried to murder, any great personage, are exceedingly painful reading. Yet, when two of the miscreants who had plotted the murder of William were arrested, he gave directions that their trial should be conducted with strict regard to the forms of law, and that no torture should be used; and after they were condemned he wrote from his sick-bed — which was likely then to have been his death-bed — requesting as a personal favour that they should not be put to any torturing death, but simply hanged like ordinary malefactors. That, under the circumstances and considering the extreme and perpetual danger of assassination in which he stood, was a heroic thing to do. It is not unconnected with our subject. You will find that it was in Protestant countries that the use of torture to extract evidence, and also of torturing aggravations of the death penalty, were earliest discontinued. Interesting details on this subject are given in Dr. Kidd's remarkable book *Social Evolution*.

We pass on to the last day of William's life. Perhaps some of us have seen, in that old house in Delft, the very room where he died. He had been dining with his family, and conversing cheerfully, as was his wont. He had left the dining-hall, and was going upstairs to the room above. As he put his foot on the third stair, an assassin, concealed in a dark alcove, fired three balls at him from a pistol. He was brought back into the dining-room and laid on a couch. His wife was there, and his sister. "God have mercy on me," he said. "God have mercy on my soul, and on this unfortunate nation!" So, to the very last, he thought of the people he had lived and was dying for. His wife — the widowed daughter of Admiral de Coligny — was overwhelmed with grief and horror, but his sister bent over him and asked, "Do you commit your soul to Jesus Christ?" He whispered "Yes," and his spirit passed.

So fell William of Orange, the founder of the Dutch Republic. In the *Apology*, which was his answer to the Ban of Philip of Spain, he had written, "God in His mercy will maintain my innocence and my honour during my life and in future days; while, as to my fortune and my life, I have dedicated both, long since, to His service. He will do what pleases Him for His glory and for my salvation."

God *has* maintained his honour and his innocence. In his own generation, where "during his life he had been the heart and soul of a great nation, and at his death the little children cried in the streets;" and also in future days, for "Never shall he be in praise by wise and good forsaken" wherever throughout the world truth, righteousness, and courage are honoured and admired; while in his own country he is still called, in grateful reverence, "Father William."

THE ROMANCE OF FAILURE I

(THE STORY OF BOHEMIA)

I shall pass, my work will fail.
— TENNYSON

The Life of

JOHN HUSS, D.D.

Johannes Hus, Martyr.
2 May: A. 1415 Combustus Mortem Obijt.
Printed for W. Parker & C. Cakewell in Cornhill London.

FROM
The Lives of the Principal Reformers
1360 – 1600

From *The Trial and Burning of John Huss*
An eyewittness account by a member of the Council of Constance

VI

THE ROMANCE OF FAILURE I

(THE STORY OF BOHEMIA)

It has been said on a former occasion that the Reformed Church of Bohemia was one of the two Protestant Churches that existed before the Reformation. It is the oldest *Reformed* Church, though not the oldest *Protestant* Church. I have recently had a letter from an eminent pastor of that Church. He had gone to Worms to attend an Evangelical Conference. On coming to the town the first thing he thought of was the Luther monument, and the first thing he did was to go, with a loving, reverent heart, to see it. But it was not to the grand figure on the apex that he looked up with the deepest love and reverence. Far dearer to his heart was one of the four which are grouped around the pedestal — Waldo, Wycliffe, Huss, and Savonarola. It was before the figure of Huss that he stood long to gaze — and it is a very beautiful one. The face — sad, yet calm and full of peace — is bent with devoutest adoration and love upon the crucifix which the sculptor has put into his hand as the symbol of Christ. My friend the pastor wrote to me, "The sculptor who designed John Huss on the Luther monument has written our Church's history in that figure. See the history of our Church — the face furrowed by pain and sorrow, but the eyes fixed with an unalterable devotion on the Crucified One — 'Though He kill me, yet will I not let Him go.' "

That was indeed the root and principle of Huss' own life, and nobly was it acted on in the two Churches of which, though he was not the founder, he was certainly the father — the present Reformed Church of Bohemia, and that "fruitful bough" whose "branches hang over the wall," the Church of the United Brethren of Bohemia and Moravia. Love to Christ and trust in Him was what John Huss lived in, and what he died for. He might have said, with Tholuck's hero in *Guido and Julius*, "I have but one passion, and that is He — He alone." Joined with this passion for Christ was its result — a passion for truth; to find the truth and to be true to the truth. "Faithful Christian," said he, "seek the truth, hearken to the truth, learn the truth, hold the truth, and defend the truth, even unto death." That might have been the motto of his own life.

But he had fallen upon evil days — very evil indeed, both for the world that called itself the world, and perhaps still more for the world that called itself the Church. We must remember that there is another side to love. If we love, our hearts *must* rise in indignation against that which would injure or destroy the object of love. It was the apostle of love who became also the "son of thunder." And well does Browning say of the great Florentine,

> *Dante, who loved well because he hated,*
> *Hated wickedness that hinders loving.*

John Huss "hated wickedness that hinders loving;" and he came into a world and a Church that were steeped in wickedness. He lived in the latter end of the fourteenth century and the beginning of the fifteenth, about a generation before the great revival of art and learning called the Renaissance, and more than a century before the Reformation. The Renaissance did not bring moral purity or renovation in its train; but undoubtedly it gilded wickedness with a superficial grace and beauty. If you read that striking poem of Browning's, "The Bishop Orders his Tomb in St. Praxed's Cathedral," you will have a wonderful picture of the Renaissance — with its art, its learning, its luxury, and also its impurity, its greed, its dishonesty. Before the Renaissance there was much of the sin, but it was for the most part without the gilding. The disorders of the time were aggravated by the great schism in the Papacy, in which at first two Popes, then actually three, contended for the tiara, each one calling himself the Vicar of Christ, and claiming "the obedience of the faithful." Happily, that is a story we have no need to tell, since we undertook to tell of the Romance of Protestantism, and we do not see that either Romance or Protestantism have much to do with it.

It was against the moral evils of the time — the "wickedness that hinders loving" — that Huss mainly contended. He was not, at first, greatly occupied with doctrine, nor indeed did he ever come to hold definitely most of the distinctive doctrines we call Protestant. He did not get so far — he had not time. But he held Christ, the centre of them all; he held also the supremacy of the Word of God, and the duty of every one to seek truth for himself, and when he has found it to hold it — which is what we now call the right of private judgment — right, on its other side, always meaning duty. Still, his message to the Church of his day was not so much, "You are preaching error: stop that in God's name," as "You are doing iniquity: stop that in God's name."

Just one story has come down to us of the early life of the widow's son of Hussenitz, the poor scholar at the University of Prague, who very probably earned his bread either by singing in the streets, as Luther did afterwards, or by hard manual labour. One winter evening the young students were sitting round the fire (in those days boys went to a university almost as early as they go now to a public school), and no doubt they were talking and laughing together as boys will do. But one sat silent, absorbed in his book, which told of the martyrdom of St. Lawrence. Presently he stretched out his hand, put it into the fire, and held it there. The others stared in amazement, till one of them had the presence of mind to seize his arm and pull it away.

"Do you want to kill yourself, John of Hussenitz?" he asked.

"I was only trying if I could bear anything of what that holy man suffered for Christ's sake," was the answer.

The eager, warm-hearted boy, so ready to prove his faith and love, grew to manhood. He became a priest, and very soon a celebrated preacher.

There are several things that we must notice, if we would understand his life-work. We have to consider his nationality, his forerunners, his instructors, his friends and his enemies. In the first place, John Huss was a Bohemian of the Bohemians. People who have not thought much about it probably suppose that Bohemia is just a province of Germany. I should like to have seen the face of John Huss if you had called him a German! The people of Bohemia are of a different race; they are not Teutons, but Slavs. They are akin to the Russians and the Poles, not to the Germans or ourselves. They had, and have to this day, a very interesting and strongly pronounced nationality. You will sometimes see in the newspapers a mention of the Czech — or "the young Czech" party (but it should be written Cěch); these are the Bohemians who wish to gain, or to regain, their national rights and privileges. In the days of Huss Bohemia was a free nation, and a strong and prosperous one. It had given Emperors to Germany. The people had not received their Christianity from Rome, but from the East, so it was rather of the Greek than of the Latin type. In the Greek Church, to the present day, the laity receive in the Lord's Supper the Cup as well as the Bread; and so the Bohemians continued to do, even long after they had submitted to the authority of the Pope. Rome crushed out that with other indications of spiritual freedom — but the love of liberty burned on. The Bohemians had also the beginnings of an interesting national literature. Their University of Prague had become celebrated, and was much resorted to by foreigners. Huss was its rector at one time: he did a great deal for the language and the literature of his country; indeed, he might almost be called their father.

Looking upon Huss, as we are used to do, as one of the forerunners of Luther, we may be surprised to hear that he had forerunners himself. In the comparative freedom of the Bohemian Church there had sprung up, just before his time, a group of good men and women who seem to have brought about a sort of revival in religion.[9]

Without any conscious departure from the dominant Church, they stirred up the embers of spiritual life that were left in it, and strove to recall men to a real faith in Christ and fear of God. One of them, a merchant and a very rich man, built a large church in Prague, which he called Bethlehem Chapel, after our Lord's birthplace. This became Huss's church, in which, while in Prague, he always preached, and

---

[9] It was from the study of the Scriptures that these "watchers of the Dawn" drew the light that was their inspiration and their strength. In the words of Pastor Vincent Dŭsek, the Bohemian pastor quoted in the text (pp. 117 and 158): "The Bible seems nowhere else to have been such a mine of instruction — from which the nation not only derived knowledge of letters in general, but also spiritual wisdom in particular — as in Bohemia." The Bible influenced directly and indirectly a vast portion of the Bohemian literature. It was the life study of Mathew of Janov, one of the forerunners of Huss. He writes of it thus: "I loved it since my youth, and called it my friend, my bride, yea, mother of beauteous delight, of learning, fear and holy hope. Wherever I moved, since my youth and till my high age, it did never forsake me, neither on my way, nor in my home, never when I was occupied, and never when I took to rest." It is said that Anne of Bohemia, the sister of King Wenceslaus, when she came to England as the bride of our King Richard II, brought with her three things, hitherto unknown there and very valuable — a side-saddle, a box of pins, and a Bible in four languages! In return, the knights and nobles, who came with her from Bohemia, brought back to their own country the writings of Wycliffe. That Jerome of Prague brought them also, or brought more of them, is quite probable.

where attentive crowds thronged to listen — not to any new doctrines that he taught, but to the message of the gospel. His preaching and teaching became a great force in the country, whether he thundered against prevailing iniquity, or told men lovingly of the love and tenderness of Christ. Where did he get the knowledge that he thus ministered to others? Chiefly from the Word of God, which, illumined by the Divine Spirit, was his constant study; in part also, no doubt, from some of his good countrymen who had preceded him; in part from the writings of our first English reformer. John Wycliffe went to his rest in 1384, when Huss was almost a child. But though he never knew him personally, he knew his writings. They were brought to Bohemia, it is said, by a scholar and a friend of his of whom we shall hear again, Jerome of Prague. Huss studied them eagerly; loved them, learned from them, reverenced them. He did not agree with Wycliffe in all things, but he felt the power of his words, and knew that they were good words. He himself acknowledges his debt in a letter which has been preserved to us, addressed to an Englishman, a follower of Wycliffe. The superscription is one which, at the present time, would strike us as a little vague — "To Richard of England" — but it evidently reached its destination. We will quote his own words, because they are a direct message from John Huss to the Christians of England: "I am thankful that Bohemia has, under the power of Jesus Christ, received so much good from the blessed land of England through your labours" — meaning through the labours of Wycliffe and of his followers. So there is a word of benediction for us of England from John Huss himself. When afterwards, before the Council of Constance, he was accused of having said that the soul of the "heretic" Wycliffe was saved, not lost, his answer was, "I said not whether the soul of John Wycliffe was saved or lost. This I said, that I would willingly have my soul where his is."

The Latin writings of Huss are said to be largely borrowed from those of Wycliffe, both in thought and in expression. But his Bohemian works are truly original, and it was through them, as well as through his preaching, that he swayed the hearts of his countrymen.

One thing which strikes us particularly in the history of Huss is that he was a man of many friends. One is constantly tempted to say, "How that man was loved!" or to call him what Daniel was called long ago, "A man greatly beloved." This runs through his whole career. At the time of his death, the University of Prague sent a letter to the Council of Constance, the words of which deserve to be remembered, no less for their beauty and their pathos than for their testimony to his character. "His life glided on before our eyes from his very infancy, and was so holy and pure that no man could find in him a single fault. O man truly pious, truly humble — thou who wast conspicuous with the lustre of such great virtues — who wast accustomed to despise riches and to succour the poor, even to the suffering of want thyself, whose place was by the bedside of the unfortunate, who movedst by thy tears the most hardened hearts to repentance, and soothedst rebellious spirits by the inexhaustible mildness of the Word . . ." So the noble panegyric flows on — much farther than we can follow it.

He was one of those good men for whom "some would even dare to die." One actually did so — that Jerome of Prague already mentioned, whose name has gone down linked with his to posterity. Jerome has been called, not inaptly, "the stormy petrel of the Reformation." We find him first a rich young noble — brilliant, gifted, eloquent, impetuous — possibly very proud of himself — hurrying over Europe from university to university, "starring it," as we should call it now. He invites learned men to dispute with him on all sorts of subjects, he puts up theses on the doors of churches and colleges, and offers to defend them, and so forth. He is enthusiastic, ardent, lovable, but wayward and fitful, and deficient in balance and self-control. This was the man who attached himself to Huss with the ardour of a young and generous nature, and learned to love and reverence him profoundly. In the end, it was not so much for any so-called heresy or error in doctrine that he died — his real heresy was that he refused to acknowledge the justice of the condemnation of Huss. He came to Constance of his own free will, in the generous hope of defending him. Huss had written entreating him *not* to come, but he would not heed him. When he came, however, and saw how things were, he took alarm, and ran away. But he was soon arrested, brought back, and thrown into prison.

Amongst the friends of Huss we may also mention his Queen, a good woman, whose confessor he was. The King, Wenceslaus, was weak and worthless, a bad man and a bad king. Swayed by passion and self-interest, he vacillated in his conduct, but may be reckoned on the whole amongst the enemies of Huss. So assuredly may the Pope, who excommunicated him and put the city of Prague under an interdict on his account. "Which of the Popes?" it may well be asked, seeing that at this time there were three — John XXIII, Benedict XIII, and Gregory XII. Of the three, John XXIII had the best title, but the worst character. Most people acknowledged the validity of his title, while his character has been well summed up in the phrase, "He was a moral monster." He was indeed one of the worst of the Popes, and that is a great deal to say. Bad as were the times, and bad as was the condition of the Church, there were those who shuddered at this state of things. Right-thinking men began to say, "We must somehow make an end of this, or all morals will be upset, and all religion too." So a great Council was summoned — a General Council — and Constance was appointed as its place of meeting. Its first object was to end the schism, and to elect a true and lawful Pope, whom all Christians might obey with a good conscience. Another object, and a most important one, was the reformation of morals, and the removal of scandals and abuses in the Church which all honest men acknowledged and deplored. There were other things too, amongst which was the desire to end the commotions that had arisen in Bohemia, where a priest named John Huss was setting every one by the ears, and preaching sedition and heresy. There were two things — the Evangelical character of his preaching, and his uncompromising denunciations of vice, especially of the vices of the Hierarchy — which drew upon John Huss the deadly hatred of the powers that then were, both in Church and State.

In November, 1414, there was a mighty stir and concourse in the little city by the lake of Constance, and in its neighbourhood. From all Europe the most illustrious people — princes, dukes, cardinals, archbishops, bishops, doctors of divinity — were flocking thither, to make this General Council as splendid and as representative as it could possibly be. The modest precincts of the town of Constance — though it must have been overcrowded to a degree that would have horrified a modern philanthropist — were quite unable to accommodate them and their attendants; so tents had to be pitched for them in the country around. Sigismund, the Emperor of Germany, was to preside over the magnificent assembly.

A magnificent assembly indeed! And yet it has been called, and we fear truly, "one of the most infamous assemblies that ever met on this earth." Amongst these great people, vice and wickedness, greed and treachery, ran rampant. Little justice indeed could be expected for any man who stood alone against that Council as a preacher of truth and righteousness! Yet we are glad to think that even that "infamous" Council had in it a few men who were *not* wicked, a few men who had come thither honestly anxious to do their duty. There were even men who gave their voices there against God's servant, and were yet sincerely desirous of serving God themselves. At least we know of one, Jean Gerson, Chancellor of the University of Paris. He was strongly opposed to Huss, and drew up certain Articles of Accusation against him. Huss said, on seeing them, "If God spares my life, I will answer the Chancellor of Paris; if I die, God will answer for me at the Day of Judgment." God *did* answer for him, and He did not wait until the Day of Judgment.

There were some Englishmen there; and the chief of them, Robert Hallam, Bishop of Salisbury, bears a good record. He was very anxious for the moral reformation of the Church, and pressed it earnestly upon the Emperor, with whom he had great influence. But he and those like him were in a small — a very small — minority.

Two men, known to us already, took their way to Constance, but with very different thoughts and feelings. John XXIII detested the Council, and dreaded it. He went there sorely against his will, but he had to go; there was no escape for him. He was justly afraid of having his misdeeds looked into, set forth and exposed, and of being deprived of the Popedom because of them. Very reluctantly he set out on his journey from Bologna, where he was at the time. When he drew near Constance his carriage broke down, and he tumbled out on the ground. "Here I lie in the devil's name," said he. No doubt he thought it a bad omen. Then, looking down the hill to the town that lay beneath, he added, "There is a fine trap to catch foxes in." And he himself, though a very wily fox, was caught in it.

John Huss had been invited by the Emperor himself to come and plead his cause before the Council. Ere he went, he wrote letters of farewell to his beloved congregation in Bethlehem Church and to his friends throughout Bohemia. In these he said that he knew not to what he was going, or whether he would see their faces again upon earth. But there was one thing which he asked them all to do — to pray for him, that he might be found "stainless." That was his one request, and History bears witness that it was granted. Huss went to the Council at the Emperor's invitation, but of his own accord. He need not have gone. With the nobles and people of Bohemia on his side he could not have been compelled. But he went willingly, for he wished to vindicate the course he had pursued and the truths he had preached. Nor did he go alone. At the express desire of his own king, Wenceslaus of Bohemia, three Bohemian nobles went with him, who were charged to look after "Master John," as they called him, and to see that he was fairly and justly dealt with. He received from Sigismund a full and complete safe-conduct — which has become famous in history. The nobles who accompanied him were John of Chlum, Wenceslaus Duba, and Henry of Latzemboch. All held him in esteem, but Chlum, the most remarkable of them, really deserves a place amongst the celebrated friends of history. He was Huss' Jonathan. Brave, devoted, unselfish, untiring, he was true to him to the very last. In the great picture of the condemnation of Huss, which is placed in the Town Hall in Prague, he stands before us, tall and stately, his face full of deep, silent, manly sorrow, and in his hand the historic hammer with which he nailed to the door of every church in Constance his protest against the deed of the Council.

Huss and his friends arrived in Constance on November 4, and lodged in the house of a widow named Fidelia, which has now a medallion on the front bearing his effigy. But after twenty-six days, he was summoned to the Franciscan Convent where the Pope was staying. Chlum and another friend went with him. They were kept for hours, Huss talking and disputing with certain persons sent to him for the purpose, and then at last Chlum was informed that he might go, but that Huss must remain a prisoner. Chlum's indignant remonstrances being in vain, he went to the Emperor and complained. But all his efforts to save his friend were fruitless. The fact was, that the Council had already determined upon his destruction. His brave witness for righteousness as well as for truth had stirred their intense hostility. He must either die as a "heretic," or retract his own words, and go back to Bohemia disgraced and powerless, unable to hurt them any more. But how was this to be accomplished? Enemies of Huss, prepared to accuse him, had already come from Prague, sent by the Papal party there. About the weight or the quality of the accusations the Council was not very particular. True or false, honest or villainous, plausible or absurd, all seemed to come alike to them. The chief accuser, whom perhaps we should call the prosecutor, Michael de Causas, seems to have been a very truculent ruffian, a man to be despised as much as hated. Huss' other great Bohemian enemy was, originally, a man of higher type. What lends pathos to the story is that Stephen Paletz had been the intimate friend of Huss. They had taken sweet counsel together and walked in the house of God as friends. Huss felt his treachery most bitterly. He could not conceal his pain when Paletz brought up fragments of their old confidential talks, things they had said to each other in openhearted friendship, and turned them against him.

Huss was now lodged in the dungeon of the Dominican Convent, which is built on a little island close to the town. The building is now a hotel, and some of us who have stayed there have stood and looked down into the depths of the dark underground dungeon where God's servant lay for months. It was a terrible place to be shut up in; the air was corrupt and noisome, for it was close to the great sewers of the monastery. The prisoner soon became very ill, but still he was left there to linger on; for it was the plan of his enemies not to have him brought to a public trial, or heard in his own defence, but to send agents to examine him secretly in prison. They hoped thus to entangle him in his talk and to make him contradict himself; and then, perhaps, they would get from him the recantation they so much desired. Yet even in that sad position the prisoner's heart did not sink. For, as was said of him truly,

> *The Saviour stood by him in pain,*
> *Nor left him in sorrow forlorn.*

We know he was strengthened and comforted, for we have many letters of his, written either from that dungeon or from another to which he was afterwards transferred. These letters are very touching. They are remarkable chiefly for the faith, the hope, the love they display, but also for their great naturalness. They are thoroughly unaffected; there is no attempt in them, so far as we can see, to appear braver, stronger, more resigned, than he was — he records the fears that crossed his mind, the conflicts he had, the times when his heart sank within him; then again he tells of the times when God drew very near him, and was indeed his light and his salvation. But perhaps the greatest characteristic of these letters is the tenderness of heart they show. Standing face to face with a cruel death, the concerns of others still occupy his mind. He thinks of all his friends, considers their welfare, enters into their cares, their concerns, and even remembers their tastes; as, for instance, in parting amongst them his very slender possessions, he will not give one intimate friend his gray coat, recollecting that he "does not like that colour." He entreats too that no one for his sake shall involve himself in any danger or loss. Certainly he had, among his other good gifts, "a heart at leisure from itself."

God gave him two comforts in his long captivity. He never seems to have had a doubt of the fidelity of Chlum and his other friends. He knew they were staunch and true, and that they were still working for him, however little they could do. And God gave him also what He gave Joseph — favour in the sight of his keepers. He won the hearts of these simple, rough, ignorant men, and they became his faithful, devoted friends. He prayed for them, he taught them, he wrote little treatises for them. The name of one, Robert, is specially recorded for the love he showed his prisoner.

After some months Huss was transferred from the prison of the Dominicans to that of the Franciscans — thence to the Castle of Gottlieben, a place about three miles from Constance, where he was brought by night in a boat, because it was feared his friends might make an attempt to rescue him. While he was there a strange thing happened. The Council had been giving its attention to the affairs of Pope John XXIII, and showing a disposition to come down upon him with a heavy hand for his sins and misdemeanours. He took alarm, and fled in dismay, dressed as a groom. But he was captured, brought back, and lodged as a prisoner in the Castle of Gottlieben. For three days John Huss and John XXIII were fellow-prisoners under the same roof. But they did not meet.

After a month in Gottlieben, Huss was brought back to the Franciscan prison, because there was a gleam of hope that, at last, the Council would consent to hear him. On the 5th of June he appeared before them for the first time. They *saw* him as he stood there, in chains like a criminal, but it can scarcely be said that they *heard* him. There was no order, no arrangement, no regard either to justice or to dignity, in their proceedings. Accusation after accusation was hurled against the prisoner. Every one who had anything to say, said it — it was simply a scene of violence and clamour. Whenever he tried to answer he was interrupted with jeers and mockery. One of the Articles of accusation against him would be read, and he would be asked whether he had said or taught so and so. He would perhaps begin: "What I said was this" — or

"That which I meant was" but a dozen voices would cry out, "Say yes or no!" Not another word would they hear from him but yes or no — scarcely that even. And when he was silent they cried out, "He has got nothing to say for himself." At last, raising his voice, he contrived to say, "I am silent, because when I speak I cannot be heard. I leave my cause to God."

The Emperor had not been present that day, but Chlum went to him and represented what had happened. He promised that the next time Huss was to be heard he would preside himself, and maintain order. He did so; and Huss was allowed to make some, at least, of his answers without interruption. But the spirit of the Council was thoroughly hostile. The great majority of its members, while they were his judges, were at the same time his bitter enemies. The so-called trial resolved itself into a struggle between the whole Council and the solitary man who stood fettered before it, strong in nothing except the consciousness of his integrity and the presence of his God. His bearing was dignified; he even ventured to say to that tumultuous assembly, "I thought that in this Council there would have been more reverence, piety, and good order." One is glad to think that the only member who put in a word in favour of the hapless prisoner was an honest Englishman. Huss was accused of denying the doctrine of Transubstantiation, which he had never done. But the Council, not choosing to accept his disclaimer, tried to entangle him in subtle questions of scholastic theology, until one of the English deputies interposed, "What is the use of all this irrelevant talk? The man believes aright concerning the Sacrament of the Altar." In the end Huss was recommended to submit unconditionally to the Council, and the Emperor himself told him that, unless he did, he himself neither could nor would protect him from the consequences of his obstinacy.

On the following day, the 8th of June, he was heard again, for the last time. He was now very ill with ague brought on by the severity of his imprisonment, and with what we should doubtless call neuralgia, which had kept him awake the whole night. But his spirit was unbroken. Amidst the storm that raged against him he stood calm and undaunted, with no touch of defiance or of boastfulness, yet "firm as the storm-stricken rock." He had nothing to retract. Some of the Articles alleged against him he could not retract, for he had never held them; others, which he *had* held, he would willingly retract, as soon as they were proved *out of Holy Scripture* to be erroneous, and not until then. At the end of that long and weary day he went forth a condemned man. He must abjure or die.

As he was being led back to prison, so exhausted that he could scarcely walk, some one pushed his way through the guards, took his hand in his, and pressed it. It was the good knight Chlum. "Oh, how sweet unto me," wrote Huss afterwards, "was the pressure of the hand of the good knight John de Chlum, who was not ashamed to stretch out his hand to me, the miserable 'heretic,' in chains, and abandoned of all men." Truly that "cup of cold water" given to Christ's suffering servant did not lose its reward.

When he wrote those words, Huss was expecting to be led without delay to the stake. He had been condemned; he had refused to retract, though pressed to do so by the Emperor himself. What else was to follow? Yet, after that, he was left in prison for a whole month, much to his surprise. This was because nearly every one desired his recantation rather than his death. The Council desired it; some — we may hope many — because his courage, his patience, and his piety had really touched their hearts; others because they thought, and truly, that his defeat and dishonour would tend much more to the glory of the Council than his death. The Emperor desired it too; because, in spite of his declaration that he could not protect a "heretic," he foresaw there would be trouble about that safe-conduct from more quarters than one, including his own conscience. So every possible effort was made to drive him from the position he had taken up, and seduce or terrify him into signing even a mild and easy form of recantation.

It must be remembered that all this time his position was not that of a modern Protestant, who having no belief at all in the sacredness or the authority of the Council, could have regarded its power to ban him with contempt, however justly he might have dreaded its power to burn him. Huss still believed that the Church of his time — though sorely defaced with iniquity and impiety, was yet the Church of Christ; and that the Council which mocked and insulted him, which thrust him forth and doomed him to infamy and death, was its authorized organ and representative. But he knew that the truths he had preached were the truths of God's Word, and therefore he could not deny them. He knew too that the falsehoods he had been accused of preaching had been never held or preached by him, and therefore it would be a falsehood of another kind to abjure them. He was emphatically a *witness for* two of the great Protestant principles — the supreme authority of the Word of God and the paramount duty of being, in both senses, "true to truth." He was not himself aware of the gulf that yawned between his own position and that of the only Church he knew. But Rome was wiser than he was. She knew he was not of her, so she cast him out and slew him. This is not the only case in which she knew her opponents better than they knew her.

But while he resisted steadfastly, though with unfailing gentleness, the attacks made upon him from without — and they were many — how was it with him in the depths of his heart, and in the solitude of his prison? It was with him, habitually, as with the man or the woman who knows God, loves God, lives in communion with God. "He that dwelleth in the secret place of the Most High" in communion "shall abide under the shadow of the Almighty" for protection. But even those who know and trust Him best have their hours of weakness; and who could always look forward without fear to the awful fate Huss was expecting? It will be found, I think, in the histories of almost all the martyrs of whom we know sufficient to trace the workings of their minds, that *before* the time of their suffering they passed through a struggle, a conflict — perhaps more than one "fearfulness and trembling took hold" of them and their hearts sank within them. But always afterwards, when the suffering actually came, they were quite calm. So with Huss. In his hour of anguish he found refuge — where we all find it — beneath the Cross of Christ. *He* had suffered — had said, "Now is my soul troubled," had been "exceeding sorrowful even unto death." "O most merciful Christ," His poor servant prayed in the dungeon of Constance, "draw us weak creatures after Thee, for except Thou draw us we are not able to follow Thee. Give us a strong spirit that we may be ready, and although the flesh is weak, let Thy grace go before us, go with us, and follow us, for without Thee we can do nothing — much less encounter cruel death for Thy sake. Give us a bold heart, an upright faith, a pure hope, and a perfect love, that we give our lives joyfully and patiently for Thy Name's sake."

His prayer was heard. Ere long the cry of joy breaks from him, "The LORD is my light and my salvation, whom shall I fear? The LORD is the strength of my life, of whom shall I be afraid?" And again, "The gracious LORD has been, and is, and I trust will be with me even to the end."

In his letter of farewell to his beloved flock of Bethlehem, he says, "When we meet again in the sweet peace of the future life, then shall you know how God has been with me through all my trials and temptations, and how He has sustained me."

In all things God gave him the victory. He had been wounded to the heart by the treachery of his old friend, Stephen Paletz, and it was not easy to forgive him. But he did it, and found a unique way of showing it. The Council, rather inconsistently, allowed him to have a confessor, and to choose whom he would. He chose Stephen Paletz, who, however, very naturally refused the office. But he visited Huss in prison. The two men, the betrayer and the betrayed, looked in each other's faces — with what feelings who can tell? Huss broke the silence. He might have said, "I die through you," but he did not. He said, "I spoke some things before the Council calculated to offend you. Will you forgive me?" At this unexpected reversal of the position, Paletz, instead of answering, burst into tears, and they wept together. Some further conversation followed, in which Paletz, much moved, urged his old friend to recant and save himself. Huss as usual refused, and Paletz went away in tears.

It was a deep grief to Huss, as it must be to every true worker, to think that his work must fail — that he had "laboured in vain, and wrought no deliverance in the earth." It is doubtful whether he ever said the words attributed to him, playing upon his name, which, in Bohemian, means goose,

Ye burn now a goose: there succeeds me a swan
Ye shall find quench your fire!

But comfort came to him in another way. One night, in his prison, he dreamed of his Chapel of Bethlehem. He had had some pictures of the Life of Christ painted on the walls for the instruction of the poor who could not read; and he dreamed that the Council, in its malice, had sent men to deface and destroy all these pictures. The people watched them, weeping and wailing; and he too was sad of heart. But the next day he went again to the chapel, and saw many painters there, who were painting many more pictures, and far more beautiful ones, "which," he adds, "I was very glad and joyful to behold. And the painters, with the people about them, said,

'Let the bishops and priests come now and put us out these pictures.' And I, awaking herewith, laughed for joy." Afterwards he thus expounds the vision: "I am no prophet, and yet I firmly hope that this image of Christ, which I engraved on men's hearts at Bethlehem where I preached His Word, will not be effaced; and that, when I cease to live, it will be far better portrayed, and by far mightier preachers, to the great joy of the people. And I too, when I awake in the Resurrection, shall rejoice thereat with exceeding joy."

On the 5th of July, the last whole day John Huss was to spend on earth, he was told that a deputation of bishops from the Council wished to see him, and he was brought up from his dungeon to the refectory to meet them. They came to make one more effort to induce him to recant. He faced them with his usual calm — but that calm was shaken utterly when he saw with them his dear friends Chlum and Duba. The Emperor himself had begged them to go to him, thinking *they* might move him. As they looked in each other's faces, Chlum said to him, "Dear Master, I'm not learned; I cannot help you by my counsel. You know whether or not you are guilty of the things of which the Council accuses you. If you are conscious of any error, do not be ashamed to yield. But if not — do not leave the path of truth for any fear of death."

Huss tried to answer him, but the look and the voice of his friend were too much, and "he whom no terror on earth could bow" broke down completely. He could only falter, "Noble lord! — oh, my beloved friend!" But, soon regaining his composure, he gave the answer he always did, both to his friends and to the bishops, and was led back to his dungeon.

Early the next morning — the morning of the 6th of July, a day remembered now in lands of which he never knew — he stood for the last time before the great Council, which was held for that occasion in the Cathedral of Constance. There they still show a white spot, which they say has remained always white and always dry since the feet of John Huss stood there, nearly five hundred years ago.

It was a splendid and imposing assembly. The Emperor sat in his chair of state, surrounded by the princes of the Empire, and by the cardinals, bishops, abbots, doctors — the deputies to the Council from all parts of Europe. All the powers, both of the Church and of the world, seemed to be arrayed to crush and destroy this one man, who, when they said to him, "Do this!" dared to answer, "*I will not.*"

For some time, while the Mass was being sung, he was kept standing outside; then the door was opened and he was led in, chained, with his guards. After a sermon by the Bishop of Lodi, came the reading of the Articles produced against him, and for which he was condemned. He requested to be allowed to answer them, but the permission was refused. Nevertheless, he managed to throw in now and then a word of explanation or remonstrance. One of these words had a far-reaching effect. He was accused of despising the Papal excommunication. "I did not despise it," he answered. "I sent my procurators to Rome, where they were ill-treated and thrown into prison. It was therefore I determined, of my own free will, to appear before this Council, under the public faith and protection of His Majesty the Emperor, here present." So saying, he looked steadily in the face of Sigismund, and a deep blush mounted to the Imperial brow. That blush of Sigismund's is thought to have saved the life of Martin Luther. "I should not like to blush as Sigismund," Charles V said at Worms.

Next was read the sentence of condemnation, which he answered by an earnest prayer that God would forgive his judges. A solemn scene followed. There had been placed in readiness, upon a scaffold, all the paraphernalia of a priest of Rome. Huss had to ascend this scaffold, and assume these things. As thus arrayed he stood before the great assembly —

a tall figure robed in priestly white and holding in his right hand the sacred chalice — he was once more adjured to recant, and accept the mercy offered him.

He answered, in a voice at first low and broken, but gathering strength as he went on, "I stand here in the presence of God, without whose reproach and that of my own conscience I could not do it. For how then could I ever lift up my face unto God? Or how could I look on the faces of that great multitude whom I have taught and instructed in His Word?"

Then came the imposing ceremony of the degradation of a priest. The insignia of his sacred office were taken from him, one by one, each with a separate curse or malediction. The last to be taken was the chalice, when these words were said, "Accursed Judas, we take from thee this cup of the Blood of the living God which thou hast profaned."

"Yet shall I drink it with Him this day, through His grace, in His kingdom," the martyr answered.

Next, the tonsure was "effaced" by cutting his hair in the form of a cross, and a hideous paper crown, covered with horrible pictures of demons, was placed upon his head.

"For the sake of my Lord Jesus Christ," he said, "who wore for me the crown of thorns, I wear with joy this crown of infamy."

At last came the words which sundered John Huss forever from that which called itself the Church of Christ. "And now the Church hath nothing more to do with thee. We give over thy body to the secular power, and thy soul to the devil." Then the Emperor, who represented the "secular power," turned to the Grand Marshall of the Empire, the Elector Palatine, and said, "Go, take him." Thus he was led forth to the place of death.

Passing out from the Cathedral, he saw, before the bishop's palace, the fire in which his books were being burned. He smiled at the sight, for he knew well they could never burn his words out of the hearts of men.

The place of death was in the Gottlieben meadow, outside the city. If you went there now, you would see the spot railed in, and marked by a great boulder all covered with ivy and other plants and flowers, bearing his name, and that of the faithful friend who suffered after him, engraved upon it. But on this day a considerable space was enclosed to keep off the people from the city, who had thronged thither in crowds.

On entering the enclosure he knelt down and prayed, "Lord Jesus, help me to bear this death of pain and shame, which for Thy Name and Word's sake I willingly encounter; and forgive all my enemies this their sin."

As the executioners led him round the space that all the people might see him, he noticed in the crowd the keepers of his prisons, the faithful Robert no doubt among them. He asked the executioners to allow him to speak to these men, and they did. He said to them, "Dear brothers, I give you great thanks for the many kindnesses you have shown me. Not my keepers have you been, but my brothers. Know also that this very day, as I steadfastly believe, I shall rejoice in heaven with my blessed Saviour, for whose Name I suffer this death."

During the long, slow, horrible preparations, he stood unmoved and calm, praying to God. At last the executioner was ready to put his torch to the faggots. Then came an interruption; two great princes riding in hot haste, sent by the Emperor to try once more if, even in the very face of death, the victim would recant and save himself. Torch in hand, the executioner paused while they pleaded with him. But with a glad voice he answered them, "I call God to witness that I have not taught anything contrary to His truth. And the truths I have taught in accordance with His Word I will now maintain, and willingly seal with my death." So the princes wrung their hands and departed.

Loving eyes however watched him to the end. Maldonowitz, Chlum's secretary, was there, and tells the story for us. As the flames rose about him the martyr prayed, "Jesus Christ, Thou Son of God, have mercy upon me!" This he said twice, and began the third time, "Jesus Christ —" but had only uttered the Name he loved, when the suffocating smoke stopped his voice. For a little space, "while you might say two or three Paternosters," his lips continued to move as if in quiet prayer. Then he bowed his head, and "departed in the Lord."

And I think we may say, as John Bunyan says of "Valiant-for-truth," that all the trumpets sounded for him on the Other Side."

THE ROMANCE OF FAILURE II

(THE STORY OF BOHEMIA CONTINUED)

What is our failure here but a triumph's evidence
For the fullness of the days?

— R. BROWNING

The Life of

JEROM of PRAGUE

Hieronimus a Praga, Martyr.
1.ᵗ Jun.ᵗ A.ᵗ 1416. Combustus: Mortem Obijt.
printed for E. Dakiwell & H. Parker, in Cornhill London.

FROM
The Lives of the Principal Reformers
1360 - 1600

From *The Trial and Burning of John Huss*
An eyewittness account by a member of the Council of Constance

VII

THE ROMANCE OF FAILURE II

(THE STORY OF BOHEMIA CONTINUED)

Our last talk closed with the close of a noble life. That end was the beginning of many things, which are not ended yet. But before we return to the land Huss loved and laboured for, we must take one more look at the guilty Council. A year later it added to its iniquities the judicial murder of his friend and pupil, Jerome of Prague, who, in his effort to save him, had become involved in his doom. Jerome underwent a long and most cruel imprisonment, until at last his faith and his courage gave way under his sufferings, and he consented to retract the opinions of Huss, and to acknowledge the justice of his condemnation. This last was the hardest thing of all for him to do, for he loved Huss as his own soul. He soon repented, and retracted his retractation. Then he had to die. As the executioner was going to light the faggots behind his back, he said to him, "Do it before my face. If I had been afraid to die, I need not have come hither." To him also is attributed a saying which we should have expected rather from the lips of his self-forgetting friend and master. Seeing a poor husbandman bringing a faggot to the pile, he is said to have exclaimed, "Oh, holy Simplicity! Thrice more guilty is he who deceives thee." But the Council had other things to do beside the condemnation of "heretics" and the suppression of heresy. It had been called together to put an end to the schism in the Papacy, and to reform the abuses of the Church. All honest men everywhere acknowledged these abuses and bewailed them. But before proceeding to reform the Church, the Council should have reformed itself — and this was just what it was neither ready nor willing to do. Many of its members were amongst the worst men in the Church, and setting the worst example. The thing they most hated and dreaded in all the world was the cry for reform, so they raised a counter cry to stop it — "We will first elect a Pope. Without that the Church is a body without a head. It can do nothing. We will have a Pope — a lawful Pope — whom all men will obey. And he will reform the Church." But the more upright amongst them feared, and with good reason, that once the new Pope got his foot in the stirrup there would be no more talk of reform. They made stout answer, "No, let us reform the Church first, and then elect a Pope, a good man, who will promise to carry out the reforms, and will keep his word." They were the best men in the Council who said this, but they were the minority. One of the foremost amongst them was our countryman, Robert Hallam, Bishop of Salisbury. His unwearied efforts for moral reform are worthy of all praise. But not quite two months after the death of John Huss he died also very suddenly: it has been said that the tragedy he witnessed hastened his own end. But I know not if this be true.[10]

Another earnest advocate for reform was Jean Gerson, the Chancellor of the Sorbonne, of whom Huss had said that if he lived he would answer his accusations, if he died God would answer for him at the Day of Judgment. Gerson's heart was true to God and to righteousness, although — as a soldier might do in the din and smoke of a battle — he had mistaken

---

[10] The Rev. Charles S. Isaacson, in his story of the English Cardinals, goes so far as to say that Hallam "almost alone among the Bishops, dissented from the condemnation of both Huss and Jerome." He was one of the Bishops sent by Sigismund to Huss on the day before his death to endeavour to persuade him to retract. Later, during the examination of Jerome, when someone cried out, "To the fire with him!" and the accused answered, "If my death is what you wish, God's will be done!" Hallam mildly interposed, "No, Jerome, it is not God's will that any sinner should die, but that he should be converted, and live."

a brother for a foe. He never ceased to press for reform, but the Council would have none of it. They turned against him — him, the champion of orthodoxy, and actually accused him of *heresy!* They could not sustain the charge — it was insult they meant and not injury — but the insult cut deep. Moreover, the year Huss died was the year of the Battle of Agincourt; and we all know that then England conquered France. Gerson, a patriotic Frenchman, felt most bitterly the humiliation of his country; and besides, he himself lost everything — his office of Chancellor and his home in Paris. It seemed as if the Church and the world had combined to crush him. He refused tempting offers of asylum and preferment from some of the princes at the Council, who respected and admired him; and, having dismissed all his attendants, he left Constance alone and on foot, in the disguise of a pilgrim. He had always esteemed himself a pilgrim and a stranger upon earth, taking his surname of "Gerson" from the Hebrew "Gershom" — "a stranger here." Thus, poor and solitary, he returned to France. He went to Lyons, where his brother was Prior of the Cistercian Monastery, and spent his last days with him, very humbly and quietly. He used to take pleasure in teaching the poor little children of the town to know and love their Saviour. Some things he said which make us think he was sorry for what he had done to Huss — such as this: "If John Huss had had proper advocates he would not have been condemned." Still more significant are other words of his: "That man who is put to death in hatred of justice and of truth, which he honours and defends, is worthy in the sight of God of the name of martyr, whatever be the judgment of man." It was a labour of love to him to teach the little children, but he asked them for a recompense. They were to say for him a short prayer, "O Lord, have pity on Thy poor servant, Gerson!" God, indeed, had pity on His poor servant — as He has on all His servants, whatever mistakes they may make. His tomb in Lyons bears the inscription, "Repent, and believe the Gospel," and also his favourite motto, "*Sursum Corda*" — "Lift up your hearts." To that voice, that speaks to us across the centuries, we make our glad response — "We lift them up unto the Lord," in thankfulness for *all* His servants who have departed this life in His faith and fear, and rest with Him now in His home above. For aught we know, John Gerson and John Huss may have met together there.

We turn back to Bohemia. There the tidings of the death of Huss called forth a wail of sorrow — yes, and a cry of indignation too which might well have "echoed to the tingling stars." All ranks, all classes united in loving his memory, and execrating his murderers. And there were many amongst the warlike barons and the stout burghers and peasantry who burned to avenge him. These sentiments ere long were intensified by persecution. For the Council proceeded to condemn the writings and the doctrines of Huss, to fulminate against those who held them, and to order their punishment. The new Pope, Martin V, confirmed the decree of the Council, and Wenceslaus, the weak and wicked king of Bohemia, let Pope and Council have their way. Then martyrdoms began; and the story of one of these shall be given, on account of the Romance in it.

The burgomaster of Leitmeritz was a bitter persecutor. He condemned a band of Hussites (as they now began to be called) to be drowned in the river, which had certainly the advantage of being a more merciful death than burning. Amongst them was a young man to whom his own daughter was betrothed. The girl had prayed her father with many tears to spare him, but he was obdurate. Then she held her peace and dried her eyes, for she thought of something she could do. When the "heretics" were bound hand and foot and thrown into the river, she watched her opportunity, slipped somehow through the line of soldiers on the bank, and swam out to her lover. With the sharp knife she had hidden in her bosom she cut the cords that bound him. She thought she could have saved him thus. But nothing more is known save that, the next morning, the two were washed ashore together — "Locked in one another's arms, and silent in a long embrace."

There were other martyrdoms too. But the people of Bohemia — like those of Holland, only more quickly — began to say to each other, "These things shall not go on." And presently they said too,

> We have steel in our hearts and our hands,
> We are thousands that fear not to die.

Eventually they took up arms; and a man arose to lead them. This was the celebrated John Ziska, "the terrible blind man." Already he had lost one eye, and he lost the other during the war, and became quite blind. But he continued to lead the army with undaunted courage and with consummate skill, and to do wonderful feats of arms. It may well be said that,

> His oaken spear
> Was true to that knight forlorn,
> When the hosts of a thousand were scattered, like deer
> At the blast of the hunter's horn.
> When he strode on the wreck of each well-fought field
> With the raven-haired chiefs of his native land,
> His lance was not shivered on helmet or shield,
> And the sword that seemed fit for archangel to wield
> Was light in his terrible hand.

Ziska of the sword, as he truly was, is called also Ziska of the Cup. The giving of the Cup to the laity in the Holy Communion had been introduced, or rather reintroduced, amongst the followers of Huss during his imprisonment. He had never done it himself; but he approved it by letter, saying it was a primitive custom and conformable to Holy Scripture. So the Cup grew rapidly to be the watchword and the symbol of his followers. Ziska had the Cup on his standard, and a gigantic Cup adorned the tower of the Tein Church, the chief church of the Hussites in Prague. It is still the emblem on the seal of the Reformed Church of Bohemia.

Over many a well-fought field, in those strange, wild years, did the Standard of the Cup wave in triumph, and the famous song of Ziska and the Cup sound forth from the victor's lips,

Soldiers of God arise,
And combat for His laws!
Implore His present help,
Maintain His holy cause!
For he who holds the Lord his friend
Must ever conquer in the end.

Dread not the foeman's might,
Nor fear his vast array!
Lift up your hearts to God,
And fight for Him this day!
No foot breadth to the foeman yield,
But die or conquer on the field.

Three crusades were proclaimed against the Hussites, and three times the brave Bohemian nation — they *were* a brave nation — made stout resistance to the invaders, and drove them back from their frontiers; they even retaliated, and invaded the German territories in their turn.

But amidst and underneath these scenes of strife and bloodshed, what we seek, and what we desire to find, are the evidences of that faith and love and loyalty to Christ in which Huss lived and for which he died. Amongst the Hussites there soon arose the two parties sure to be found in free communities — the party that wanted to stop, and the party that wanted to go on. These were called respectively Calixtines and Taborites — the Calixtines from Calix, a cup — the giving of the Cup to the laity being the reform they most desired; also the acknowledgment of the supremacy of the Holy Scriptures, and the free preaching of the Word of God — if these were granted them, they had no wish to separate from Rome. The Taborites went much farther — as far, it seems, as we Protestants do now. They got their name from a hill called Mount Tabor, which was in the midst of a district where Huss used to preach, and the people were devoted to his doctrines. Mount Tabor became a gathering-place whither multitudes used to flock, and to hold great Revival meetings, as we should call them now — only these were monster meetings indeed, like ten or twenty rolled together. Mount Tabor itself and the district around it would be filled with the crowds of people, and many seem to have encamped and stayed there permanently. We cannot doubt that it was the scene of a genuine Revival, though there was also, as was inevitable under the circumstances, an admixture of wild excitement and of fanaticism. There sprang up in the minds of these persecuted people a thought — a hope — which has often throughout the Church's history been sent to her in times of special trial and difficulty. They looked for the Second Coming of Christ. They believed it *must* be near — and it *might* be immediate. Any day, any hour the heavens above them might open, and then they would see Him — Him whom their souls loved,

The Lamb for sinners slain;
Redeemer, King, Creator,
In bliss return to reign.

But the heavens did not open, as we know. They have not opened yet. Nearly five hundred years have passed away since those men of Bohemia looked for Him, watched for Him, waited for Him, and died in faith, "not having received the promise." And still we watch and wait — crying to Him often, "Lord, behold, the world which Thou lovest is sick — wilt Thou not come and save it?" And still He "abides in the place where He is," — not two days, but nigh upon two thousand years. Yet for those who, *loving His appearing*, have died, or have still to die in faith, there is nothing lost. For each of these Death is but the messenger whom the Master "sends to fetch the willing one home. The same preparation suffices for both, and the loving heart is satisfied with either." Yes, and in His own time the whole Church shall be satisfied too.

We have a curious and interesting glimpse of these Taborites, as seen from the outside. They were once honoured by the visit of a Cardinal, the learned, accomplished, and amiable Æneas Sylvius Piccolomini, afterwards Pope Pius II. The Cardinal, travelling for his amusement, happened to find himself near Mount Tabor, and felt curious to see what these Bohemian Hussites were like. So he paid them a visit, and was received not only with the utmost courtesy, but with warm and openhearted hospitality. They supplied all his wants, and won from him an unstinted meed of praise. He bore witness that these peasants in ragged frocks "showed the good manners and the courtesy of nobles and of princes." As time passed on there were many troubles, and much contention between the Calixtines and the Taborites. Rome tried to attract the Calixtines to herself by a few concessions, soon to be withdrawn; and she was in great measure successful. She even induced them to join her in persecuting the Taborites. Yet all the time those that in both parties feared the Lord and clung to Christ above all things "spake often one to another." They even began to unite, and to call each other Brethren. They were chiefly amongst the Taborites, but no doubt some of the Calixtines joined them also; and one of the Archbishops of Prague, named Rockyzana, was their friend, though a rather lukewarm one. But he had a nephew named Gregory, an earnest, devoted man of God, who was to him as a son.

At one time, in Prague, a partial persecution arose against these Brethren, who were accused, quite falsely, of disloyalty to the King. Gregory, who chanced to be in the city, was present at a devotional meeting which was broken in upon by the magistrates, and those present taken to prison. Here they were put to the torture, to wring from them the evidence of political designs which in fact did not exist. Gregory was racked so cruelly that he fell into a death-like swoon.

Meanwhile the Archbishop, who had been ignorant of the whole, was told by some one of the danger of his nephew. In much distress he rushed off to the prison, and saw his kinsman, as he thought, lying dead. With tears and lamentations he bewailed him, crying out in his anguish, "Would to God I were with thee, my Gregory!"

But Gregory was not dead, nor his work done yet. He recovered, and resumed his position as a leader amongst his brethren. He obtained for them from his uncle the gift of the Castle of Lititz with the surrounding district. To this lonely place, the safer for its loneliness, those who sought a pure faith and a simple worship thronged from other parts of Bohemia, and also from Moravia. There they found shelter from persecution, brotherly communion and sympathy, and opportunity for the study of God's Word and for prayer.

They soon began to say to one another, "We no longer belong to the Church of Rome; but some Church, some organization we ought to have. We ought also to have a regular Ministry, duly ordained to administer the Sacraments and to preach the Word of God, and we wish to have bishops, presbyters, and deacons, as there were in the early days of the

Church." But how were they to accomplish this? "We must get," they said, "some one who has himself been consecrated as a bishop to consecrate two or three of our brethren, who will then be our bishops, and ordain our pastors for us." So, after much deliberation, they chose out nine of their most saintly and eminent members. Then they took twelve slips of paper, on three of which they wrote the word *est*; the rest they left blank. They put in the three extra slips because they said, "If God does not wish us to proceed farther in this matter, He will cause the three *ests* not to be drawn." They gave the bag with the papers to a little boy who did not know the meaning of what he was doing, and told him to give one to each of the nine men. All the three *ests* were drawn, and by excellent men, well suited to the office they were destined for. They did actually receive consecration as bishops, at the hands, as it would appear, of two Waldensian bishops who belonged to a colony of Waldenses settled in Moravia. This was the formal beginning of the Church of the United Brethren of Bohemia and Moravia, which has rendered such faithful, loving, devoted and heroic service to God and to His cause. From amidst the turmoil and confusion of that evil time it arose pure and peaceful, as the dove from the heap of refuse with "her wings covered with silver and her feathers with yellow gold."

During the remainder of the fifteenth century and part of the sixteenth, the Church of the United Brethren — or the Church of the Unity, as it was commonly called — endured much persecution. One story of that time I should like to tell. The Brethren had a bishop named John Augusta, a born leader of men, with great abilities, untiring energy and splendid virtues, though not quite without what the French would call "the defects of his qualities." The Emperor Ferdinand I, whom we know already as the brother and successor of Charles V, was also King of Bohemia. He was a bigot and a persecutor, and his hatred of the Bohemian Protestants was aggravated by the suspicion (unjust, as we believe) that they were plotting to dethrone him, and to make our friend, John Frederick the Great-hearted, king in his place. Augusta was the special object of his wrath, but he did not find it easy to get him into his power, so well was he sheltered by his devoted flock. At last however, by means of a plot devised by one Schöneich, with what has been truly called "Satanic treachery," he and his deacon Bilek were both arrested. They were brought to the "White Tower" in Prague, where both of them were tortured, and with the most horrible and ingenious cruelty. The accounts of the bishop's sufferings will indeed scarcely bear perusal. He endured them with splendid heroism, refusing steadfastly to deny his Faith, to confess a treason of which he knew himself innocent, or to say a word which could imperil any of his brethren. When asked what they were doing, his answer was, "They are seeking refuge everywhere in impassioned prayer to God." Bilek also behaved with very noble constancy. Twice over were the cruel tortures repeated, till both the victims were left almost dead, though still unsubdued in spirit.

The grand old castle of Pürglitz, about twenty-five miles west of Prague, stands on the top of its conical hill, girded around by lesser hills covered with dense forests. To this fortress-prison, for what reason we know not, the exhausted sufferers were brought, weak as they were, and covered with horrible, untended wounds. They were brought in separate wagons, so they had not even the consolation of exchanging a word or a look; and on their arrival they were thrust into separate dungeons. Small as were the windows of these cellars, they had been carefully blocked up, so that all the light that came into each was through an opening *four inches square*. For years they never left their dungeons; they never saw each other's faces. They never saw anyone, indeed, except the gaoler and the guard. Their imprisonment lasted, in the bishop's case sixteen, in Bilek's thirteen years — happily not in all its horrors all the time.

A frequent visitor to Pürglitz was the Archduke Ferdinand, the Emperor's son, who came to hunt in the forest that surrounded the castle. Some years before, this young prince, on a visit to Augsburgh, saw on a balcony the fair face of Philippine Welser, daughter of one of the famous "merchant princes" of that city. He saw — and he loved, with an honourable, constant, chivalrous love. The Emperor stormed, the Court lifted up its hands in horror at the mésalliance. Nevertheless, though not until after much delay and many difficulties, the Emperor's son and the merchant's daughter were wedded, and lived together most happily. The Archduchess Philippine,

> *Shaped her heart with woman's meekness*
> *To all duties of her rank,*

and has left behind her a fragrant memory, which lingers still. At last, in a good hour for the prisoners of Pürglitz, the Archduke brought her with him there.

The story of the bishop and his companion awakened in her compassionate heart a great pity, not unmixed with reverence. She showed them every kindness in her power; she even made, then and afterwards, earnest endeavours to procure their liberation. But for that the time was not yet. When Easter drew on — the Easter of 1561 — she came herself to the bishop's dungeon, and asked him what he desired most by way of an Easter boon, promising to get it for him if she could.

In answer, the bishop prayed that he and Bilek might be permitted to spend the Easter festival together in fellowship and in freedom, reminding her that the Roman governor of old was wont to release a prisoner at the Passover Feast. She promised it should be done; and then she went, with the same inquiry, to the dungeon of Bilek. He asked for the same boon as the bishop, and almost in the same words; which surprised her greatly, for she knew there could not have been any communication between them. She herself was going to Prague to spend Easter there with her husband, and she obtained his permission for the favour. Her letter to the governor announcing it came to Pürglitz on Good Friday. He happened, when he received it, to be in the dungeon of Bilek. He told him the good news, and led him out himself into the courtyard, where two chairs had already been placed. He bade him sit down.

"How long is it since you have seen the bishop?" he asked.

"It is eight years," said Bilek.

"Would you know him if you saw him?"

Before he answered, Bilek looked up. Two were approaching — the governor's wife and the bishop, with his white hair, worn frame, and feeble step. The next moment he and Bilek were locked in each other's arms, with a gush of happy tears. The governor and his wife wept with them. There, in the fresh air and under the open sky, which for so long they had not seen, they were allowed two blessed hours together; but their promised days of grace did not begin until Easter Sunday. For that day, and the two that followed, they were allowed the freedom of the castle, and treated by the governor as guests. With such dignity, courtesy, and modesty did they bear themselves that they won all hearts; and when they had to return to their dungeons they were not the only ones to regret it. From that time their captivity was softened in many ways; but weary years had yet to pass before the obdurate Emperor would yield to the pleadings of his son and grant their release. However, it *was* granted at last, and they died among their own people.

The Emperor Ferdinand I was succeeded, both as Emperor and King of Bohemia, by his son, Maximilian II, an enlightened and amiable prince, under whom the Churches had rest. The latter part of the sixteenth and the early part of the seventeenth century were the halcyon days of Bohemian Protestantism, and indeed of Bohemian nationality.

The Church of the Unity was the most numerous and the most active Protestant Church in the country. But it was not the only one. The Lutheran and the Reformed Churches were also largely represented there. So the three Communions very wisely made a "concord" or alliance together; they were not one, but they were united in faith, hope, and charity; and thus they were enabled to live together in peace, and to pursue the work of God in harmony. They were at this time the majority, probably the great majority, of the nation. A golden age for Bohemia seemed to be beginning; the country grew in wealth and prosperity, in art, in literature, and in learning — above all, in the best kind of learning.

Our great Reformer, Tyndale, when he resolved to translate the Bible, boasted that he would make "the boy that driveth the plough" know more of religion than those who were then the Doctors of Divinity. It was said that in Bohemia at that time the boy that drove the plough could not only read the Bible in his own tongue, but could read it in Latin also, and take his part intelligently in any dispute about its meaning. Men may have thought then — probably they did think — that Bohemia was destined to take a high place in the coming age and to fulfil a noble destiny. But this was not to be. A great curse fell upon the land, destroying all its progress in the present, all its hope for the future. And so the glory departed, never since to return.

Some years ago the river upon which Prague is built — the Moldau — overflowed its banks, and a good deal of damage was done. Our friend the Bohemian pastor mentioned before, wrote to us about it, telling how the beautiful Bridge of Prague, adorned with splendid statues, had been broken; but he added, with evident satisfaction, that not one of the statues was carried away by the flood except that of Ignatius Loyola, "the *scorch* of Bohemia." He meant to say "the *scourge* of Bohemia," but, though he writes English exceedingly well for a foreigner, he made a slip there. Yet it only brought him nearer the truth. The Jesuit was a "scorch" more than a "scourge" by so much as the anguish and the destruction of fire are worse than the blows of the scourge or the rod.

After the good and wise Emperor Maximilian came his son Rudolph, a dreamer and astrologer, who took little interest in the affairs of State. After him again came Mathias, who died childless, nominating as his heir his cousin Ferdinand. This Ferdinand was the pupil and the tool of the Jesuits; they had him soul, body, and estate. The Bohemians had obtained a charter guaranteeing their liberties, civil and religious. It was called the *"Majestäts Brief"* or "Letter of Majesty," and they looked upon it very much as we do upon Magna Charta. But Ferdinand, under the baneful influence of the Jesuits, began to violate its provisions, one after the other, and especially to oppress and persecute the Protestants. They bore it for a time, but the sons of Ziska and his Hussites were brave men, strong of heart and hand. They remonstrated, and their remonstrances were disregarded. Then they formed a League for the preservation of their liberties. At last came the outbreak. The League sent its deputies to bring their grievances before the Council of Ferdinand in Prague, and to demand justice from it. This Council, composed of the tools and ministers of Ferdinand, called "Regents," sat in a high chamber of the Hradschin, the palace and fortress of Prague. Thither came the deputies, forcing the unwilling doorkeeper to open to them. So they stood face to face with their enemies — the worst of these being two nobles, Martenitz and Slavata, who had been cruel oppressors. The deputies did not spare them their reproaches. The nobles retorted, and a furious altercation ensued. Deeds followed words. Some one voiced the name of an old Bohemian method for getting rid of obnoxious persons with speed and sureness — *Defenestration*. It comes from the Latin *fenester*, a window. "To the window! — To the window!" angry voices shouted. Martenitz and Slavata were seized in spite of their desperate resistance, dragged each to a window and flung down to the depth below. Their secretary, Fabricius, was flung after them to keep them company.

You think they were killed by the fall? Not they! There chanced to be a heap of refuse just beneath the window; so they fell soft, and were not much hurt, save that Slavata in falling struck his head against the wall. This extraordinary preservation the Roman Catholics attributed to the grace of the Virgin, the Protestants to the power of the devil. The three men escaped from the country, not without the aid of some kind-hearted Protestants. The secretary, Fabricius, was afterwards ennobled by the Emperor, who gave him the appropriate title of Baron von Hohenfall — Lord Highfall!

The *Defenestration* of the Regents took place on May 23, 1618, and that day stands marked in history for evermore as the beginning of the great "Thirty Years' War." Since that was a war between Protestants and Roman Catholics, it pertains to our subject on one side; while on the other the element of Romance is by no means absent, centring chiefly around the career and character of the Protestant hero, Gustavus Adolphus. But we must confine our thoughts to Bohemia.

The flood-gates of war were opened now. Protestant Bohemia threw off the yoke of Ferdinand and the Jesuits, and exercising her ancient right of electing her sovereign, chose for herself a Protestant king — Frederick, Elector of the Palatinate. Frederick's mother was the daughter of William the Silent, and what is of still more interest to us — his wife was the daughter of James I of England, and the sister of Charles I. It is through her descendants that the crown has come down to King Edward VII.

Between the hosts of Ferdinand and those of Frederick a terrible battle was fought, at a place near Prague, called the White Mountain. It ended, for the Bohemians, in utter disaster. It was indeed one of those events in history which tempt us to ask, with the poet,

> O righteous Heaven, ere freedom found a grave,
> Why slept the sword, omnipotent to save?
> Where was thine arm, O Vengeance, where thy rod,
> That smote the foes of Zion and of God
> That crushed proud Ammon, when his iron car
> Was yoked in wrath, and thundered from afar?
> Where was the storm that slumbered till the host
> Of bloodstained Pharaoh left their trembling coast,
> Then bade the deep in wild commotion flow,
> And heaved an ocean on their march below?

These are questions for which we have no answer — *yet*. But we know there *is* an answer, and we know that we shall find it — in the day of "the revelation of the righteous judgments of God."

Bohemia lay now at the feet of Ferdinand and of the Jesuits. Their reign began with the trial and execution of twenty-seven of the most distinguished men in the kingdom of Bohemia. It was as if some foreign nation conquered England, and immediately sent to the scaffold, for the crime of having resisted the invaders, all the Ministry of the day, with the heads of the Opposition to keep them company, and the foremost men of the great professions, of science and of literature, to complete the tale. The victims were most of them old men — one of them was eighty-six, others over eighty. They had all served their generation well, some with signal distinction.

Sixteen of the twenty-seven belonged to the Unity, ten to the Reformed or Lutheran Churches, and one was a Roman Catholic. But the whole of that illustrious band, without a single exception, died in steadfast faith and in holy peace. During their imprisonment they were continually beset by the Jesuits, who not only tried by every argument they could think of to shake their faith, but tempted them by offers of mercy to forsake it. Not one of them yielded a hair's breadth; and, what was strange, the single Roman Catholic amongst them rejected the ministrations of the Jesuits, and expressed his simple faith in the salvation of Christ. No pastor of the Unity was allowed to visit them in prison, but some Lutheran pastors were permitted to do so, and these, on the last day of their lives (Sunday, June 20, 1621), gave them the tokens of the dying love of Him whom they were so soon to see. All partook joyfully, except Dionys Czernyn, the Roman Catholic, who stood apart with tears in his eyes. The rest invited him to join, but he did not feel free to do so. "I am satisfied," he said, "with what I have in my heart," meaning that he had Christ there.

Next morning, in the *Grosse Ring* of Prague, the solemn sacrifice of blood was offered. As one by one each victim left his fellow-sufferers to mount the scaffold, he spoke words of faith and hope which have been carefully preserved.

"I now venture to die for Christ," said one. "Do Thou, Lord Jesus Christ, receive my soul!" said another. "Do Thou, O Sun of Righteousness, grant that I may, through the shadow of death, come to Thy Light," prayed a third. So was it with them all. The one Name was on every lip; the one trust was in every heart. All the salvation, all the desire of these illustrious Bohemians of three hundred years ago, could not be better summed up than in the simple words which the brave men who died the other day in that coal-mine of Hamstead wrote beneath their names, "We are trusting in Christ."

Through the yesterday of ages,
Jesus, Thou hast been the same,
Through our own life's chequered pages,
Still the one dear, changeless Name.

That first holocaust was followed by seven terrible years of misrule, oppression, and cruelty. At the end of those seven years Ferdinand boasted that there was not a Protestant left in Bohemia. But then, when those years began, the population of the country was about five million: when they ended, it was not more than eight hundred thousand. This was the work of the Jesuits — and it was worthy of them!

Of course the Church of the Unity was broken up. The pastors were banished — when they were not slain; and the people emigrated — when they could. They had at this time for their presiding bishop a very eminent man, John Amos Comenius. His ability was remarkable, and his learning not less so; he wrote many books, especially on the subject of education, about which he was an enthusiast. He had now to leave the country he loved, and he did it with a breaking heart. As he traversed the mountains that separate Bohemia from Germany, he came to the spot whence, for the last time, Bohemia could be seen. There he knelt down, and prayed that the Word of God in that land might never be extinguished, but that it might burn on from generation to generation. And it has. In spite of Ferdinand's boast he had *not* killed Protestantism — it is the very hardest thing in the world to kill — in Bohemia it lived on; and it lives on yet, thank God.

But when Comenius reached the land of his exile, his heart was sore and bitter within him. He thought that the Church of which he was the head — the beloved Church of the Unity — was dying, without earthly hope of revival. And so, very sorrowfully, he wrote, *The last Will and Testament of the*

Church of the United Brethren. But years passed away. As he grew old and patient, he learned more of God's will and ways, and then he came to think that the Church of the Unity was *not* dead — that God would not let it die. *He* was dying; but his Church would live on. So instead of the Church's Testament, he wrote his own. He bequeathed the Church as a precious and sacred legacy — and to whom? Let us hear his own words. "To you our friends (*the Church of England*) we leave and commit . . . our dear Mother, the Church herself. Whether God will deem her worthy to be revived in her native seats, or let her die there and resuscitate her elsewhere, in either case do you in our stead care for her. Even in her death, which seems to be approaching, you ought to love her, because in her life she has gone on before you, for more than two centuries, with examples of faith and patience." He reminds the Church of England that the Church of the Unity is one with her in doctrine and in discipline, having the three Apostolic Orders — bishops, presbyters, and deacons.

So the Church of which Huss was the spiritual father was actually bequeathed to the Church of England. But, sad to say, the bequest was never claimed. It lay unheeded; it was allowed to lapse.

After some sixty years however, one arose to claim it. God had touched the heart of a rich young noble of Saxony, not only to believe in Christ for his own salvation, but to lay all he was and all he had unreservedly at His feet. Count Zinzendorf had but one thought, one aim — how to serve Him best. He read the book of Amos Comenius which contained the bequest. With a thrill of solemn joy the thought came to him that *this* was the work Christ meant him to do, and for which He had been preparing him. So he knelt down and, as in His presence, registered his vow: "Though I have to sacrifice my earthly possessions, my honours and my life — so long as I live, and as far as I shall be able to provide, even after my death, for such a consummation — this little company of the Lord's disciples shall be preserved for Him, until He comes."

Nobly did he keep his word. In Bohemia and Moravia the "Hidden Seed," as it was called, however oppressed and persecuted, had never ceased to exist. In secrecy and suffering many men and women continued to hold the Faith they loved. The Jesuits were untiring in their efforts to seize and burn every Protestant book, especially every Bible or part of the Bible they could find — and to punish the possessors with severity. But in vain. They could not burn the words of God out of the hearts of the people. Great were the stirrings of heart, and wild the throbbings of new hope, amongst this sorrowful remnant, when the news passed secretly from lip to lip that God had raised up a friend for them at last — that if they could only make their way across the mountains to Saxony they would find a welcome there, and a place which a rich nobleman had prepared on purpose to receive them. So they came by twos and threes, and sometimes in larger numbers, across the Saxon mountains from Bohemia, and from other countries also, to this new Land of Promise. So began the settlement of Herrnhut. At first it looked a dreary solitude, but very soon, under the willing hands of the happy and grateful exiles, it began to rejoice and blossom as the rose. It became the cradle of the resuscitated Church of the Unity — that splendid missionary Church which has done so much for God and for His cause, and has been foremost in the blessed work of gathering in the heathen. The great martyr Church of the past is the great missionary Church of the present. It is said that one in every sixty of the members of that Church is a missionary. These — with those who came before and shall follow after — are the "Painters" Huss saw in his prophetic vision, who are painting the image of Christ upon the hearts of men in countries he never knew or heard of. May God bless abundantly all their work for Him, and may He bless also His faithful servants in the land of their fathers! There also they are a living Church, growing and spreading. They cherish fondly and proudly the memories of their heroic past; and we believe they are earnestly desiring and seeking to "follow those who through faith and patience have obtained the promises." May God's blessing rest upon both the branches of this ancient Church — the oldest Reformed Church in existence — upon that which is still rooted in its native soil, and upon the fruitful bough which "hangs over the wall!"

And for ourselves — can we conclude with better words than those of the Moravian Easter Morning Litany? — "Keep us in everlasting fellowship with our brethren and our sisters who have entered into the joy of their Lord, and with the whole Church triumphant: and let us eternally rest with them in Thy presence.

"Glory be to Him who is the Resurrection and the Life; He was dead, and behold! He is alive for evermore; and he that believeth in Him, though he were dead, yet shall he live.

"Glory be to Him in the Church which waiteth for Him, and in that which is around Him, for ever and ever! Amen."

THE HINDRANCES TO THE WITNESS

We know the arduous strife, the eternal laws
To which the triumph of all good is given.
— WORDSWORTH

William & Mary Trilogy, Volume 3

For God and the King

INHERITANCE PUBLICATIONS

NEERLANDIA, ALBERTA, CANADA
PELLA, IOWA, U.S.A.

King William III - Prince of Orange

The last of the great Reformational heroes of Protestantism

From *For God and the King*
by Marjorie Bowen, Author of *I Will Maintain*

VIII

THE HINDRANCES TO THE WITNESS

There is a beautiful Greek legend about the Battle of Marathon, where the heroic bands of Greece drove back from her shores the hordes of Asia — and Greece at that time stood for freedom, for thought, for progress, for civilization. It is said the fight was won not so much by the living as by the dead — that conspicuous in the van there rode,

> *A leader crowned*
> *And armed for Greece that day,*
> *But the falchions made no sound*
> *On his gleaming war array.*
> *In the battle's front he stood,*
> *With his tall and shadowy crest;*
> *But the arrows drew no blood,*
> *Tho' their path was thro' his breast.*
> *Far sweeping thro' the foe,*
> *With a fiery charge he bore,*
> *And the Mede left many a bow*
> *On the sounding ocean shore*
> *And the field was heaped with dead,*
> *And the sails were crowded fast,*
> *As the sons of Asia fled,*
> *When the shade of* Theseus *passed.*

So the dead fought and conquered for freedom and for Greece. Now, in our great battle we have not only one dead hero fighting for us, but a hundred — no, a thousand. We have heroic memories of the past, glorious thoughts for the present, splendid hopes for the future. Then why does not victory crown our standards? Why are not our fields "piled with dead" — dead errors, delusions, superstitions? What stops the way? Where are the hindrances? For hindrances there must be and perhaps if we recognized them we might help to remove them.

The first hindrance we shall name is our ignorance. Not our *general* ignorance — far from it! Protestants, as compared with others, are not ignorant. No; we have ever been the friends of knowledge, of literature, and of science. I think we shall find that Protestants in the past have been foremost in opening up the treasures of these to mankind, and that in the present we have in Protestant countries more education, more enlightenment, more activity of thought than elsewhere.

At the time of the Revocation of the Edict of Nantes, when such Protestants as were not heroes and martyrs in heart were forced into the Church of Rome, some of these "new converts" went to the priests and said, "Teach us about your religion. You have made us Roman Catholics, now we want you to explain to us the Roman Catholic faith. What are your doctrines? What do you mean by this, that, and the other which you tell us to do?" The poor curés wrote to their bishops in much perplexity, "Here are these Protestants asking us to *teach* them. What are we to do? We have not been in the habit of thinking that our people needed instruction of that kind." Protestantism awakens the mind, teaches men to think, stirs in them the desire for instruction. Romanism as a rule does not.

With ourselves, in these modern days, the difficulty is not that we know so little, but that our sphere of knowledge is so vast. The fields that open before our mental vision are so wide, so far-reaching, so boundless, that it has become impossible for us to explore them all — we are obliged to specialize, to take up, some one thing and some another. Perhaps the utmost to which anyone can aspire is to know a little about everything, and to know a great deal about one thing. And it has happened somehow that amidst all our knowledge, all our learning extending over a hundred fields, one particular field has been overlooked. Not the field of history as a whole, but an important part of it. Pity it is that in our great public schools[11] the young, who will by and by be the leaders of our thought and the pioneers of our progress, are taught much about the siege of Ilium, but little about the sieges of Leyden and Londonderry; much about the noble three hundred that died at Thermopylæ in obedience to the sacred laws of Sparta, but little of the yet nobler three hundred who died in England during five short years, in obedience to the higher law of Christ their King. Far too much neglected has been the study of our Church history, and especially of our Protestant Church history. If only a few young minds — a few young hearts already devoted to Christ their King — would give themselves to that noble and most instructive branch of historical study, I think they would do great service to God and man, and I know they would be amply repaid.

On account of our ignorance, there are very few of us who have a proper grasp of this subject, or a true and wide outlook. One of the results is seen in the vague and misty way in which many people talk upon the subject of religious persecution. We have touched upon this point in a former talk, when we recalled the well-known name of Michael Servetus, who was undeniably burned by Protestants, and burned for his religious opinions. We have shown how this question of

---

[11] The reader should bear in mind that this book was written during the first few years of the 20th century. — Editor.

persecution appears when resolved into one of proportion. May I be allowed to illustrate, even by a rather ludicrous comparison, the difference, in this matter of proportion, between our record and that of Rome? A lady once said to Beau Brummell, "Mr. Brummell, do you never eat vegetables?" "Yes, Madam," was the answer, "*I once ate a pea*." We confess to having eaten that pea![12]

Forgive even the semblance of a jest upon a matter so tragically serious.

Intolerance is the principle of Rome and the logical outcome of her creed. Her own adherents, when they are candid, avow this themselves, and we respect them for their honesty. They say to us, "You are bound to tolerate us because it is your principle; but we are not bound to tolerate you, because it is against our principle!" And the *Tablet*, the great Roman Catholic newspaper, once put the matter, from its own point of view, with admirable force and directness. "Rome is intolerance itself, because she is the Truth itself."[13]

---

[12] We regret to state that in England, during the reign of Edward VI, Joan Bocher and another — a man named Paris — were also burned for Unitarianism.

[13] It may be worth while to let another Roman Catholic authority speak for his Faith and himself. In a pamphlet on "Liberty of Conscience," published by the Catholic Truth society, Monsignor Croke Robinson says: "How could the Catholic State allow this so-called Liberty of Conscience? As well might you ask a person to allow poison to be introduced in his body. Do you say, What a cruel and bigoted thing for the Catholic Church and state to put down Heresy? We only ask you to allow the Catholic state the right no man will deny himself and his neighbour, to reject poison from his system." And again: "If tomorrow the Spanish Government, as advised by the Catholic Church, were to see that a greater evil would ensue from granting religious liberty than from refusing it, then it would have a perfect right to refuse it. Of course the Protestant press would team with charges of Intolerance, and we should reply, Toleration to Protestants is Intolerance to Catholics."

To which reply the proper rejoinder would be: "Very well; then you force us Protestants no longer to tolerate you. Not from bigotry, not from inhumanity, but from the first law of life — the law of self-preservation." Yet it is our glory that we need not, and do not, answer thus. We are not driven to invert your own hateful maxim and say that "Toleration to Catholics is intolerance to Protestants." We hold the purer Creed, the higher Law, and we own the duties it imposes on us. We give

Really, there is something sublime about that sentence! When Rome falls, it will certainly not be because she is illogical, nor yet because she is inconsistent. Her deductions in this instance are quite logical, and she has acted upon them with marvellous consistency. It is only her premises that are in fault. She has erected an imposing structure, put together with admirable skill and elaborately adorned; all it lacks is — a foundation.

It is an article of her creed, universally taught, insisted upon, and "required to be believed" of all men, and women too, who join her communion, that out of her own pale there is no salvation. Once that is granted, every violence, every cruelty, is justified which can keep men and women and children from falling into the terrible gulf of hopeless perdition that yawns outside.

The Inquisitor's maxim, "In this case cruelty is mercy, and mercy is cruelty" was, from his point of view, indisputable. He and the Church whose agent he was, violated no rule of logic; but they violated something else: they violated the first law that makes civilized life a possibility — that which goes by the name of the "social contract." If, in a war, one of the belligerents absolutely refuses to give quarter, what is the other to do?

"No quarter" has ever been the principle of Rome in her conflict with Protestants. It was a war of extermination. Wherever Rome prevailed death or conversion was the law — often indeed the practice was death without the chance of

---

you full Toleration, full civil and religious liberty. No, we are willing to do, and have often done, much more — if you are hungry we will feed you, if you are thirsty we will give you drink. But one thing, God helping us, we will *not* do. We will put no sword into your hands to slay us, since it is your avowed intention to do it if you can.

And to our fellow-Protestants we are bound to say: Let us walk in love, but let us also walk in wisdom. Let us beware — as in the sight of God — how we give power, political, moral, or material, into hands pledged to use it against us and against those who hold our Faith.

conversion. Every Protestant was like a man who feels a murderer's grip on his throat. Is he intolerant if he strikes the murderer back again as hard a blow as he can? We acknowledge that religious toleration *as a theory* was not understood at the time of the Reformation, nor long after, save by a few enlightened spirits, such as William the Silent and Henry IV of France. But in spite of the frequent mistakes and the occasional crimes which are inseparable from fallible humanity, there was between the two parties a great moral contrast, which we will try to illustrate.

During the wars of religion in France a soldier of fortune, named Des Adrets, joined the Huguenots, and held a command under Admiral Coligny. He was a brutal, hardhearted-man, with no real religion, having joined the Protestant party out of personal enmity to the Guises. He committed various excesses — amusing himself, for instance, by forcing his prisoners to throw themselves from the top of a high tower. But these cruelties aroused the indignation of the other Protestant leaders, and, on their being reported to Coligny he deprived him of his command. Des Adrets returned eventually to the Roman Catholic faith and the Roman Catholic party.

About the same time one of the Roman Catholic generals, named Montluc, committed a series of frightful barbarities, of which sickening accounts remain to us, some of them from his own pen. And to one of these stories a Roman Catholic historian adds: "The cruelty was excessive, even to killing infants in the arms of their mothers, and the mothers after them." Was this monster disowned, or punished, or even reprimanded for his atrocities? They were well known in high quarters, even in *the highest*. And they brought him a letter from no less a person than the Pope — the so-called Vicar of Christ. "Very noble and well-beloved son, health and Apostolic benediction," so it began, going on to the most fulsome and extravagant praises of his deeds, "works of a most true

Christian and Catholic, and, without doubt, excellent gifts conferred by Heaven." His Holiness adds that after former good service under earthly kings and princes, he is now called on to "maintain, with still greater glory, honour, and reputation, the war of the King of kings, Jesus Christ, and fight the fight of the Lord of Hosts. For this thou mayest assure thyself that His eternal favour will never fail thee," and so on, and so on. Did ever blasphemy of infidel profane the Name that is above every name as hideously, as cruelly, as this letter of him who dared to call himself His Vice-regent?[14]

---

[14] It may be worth while to give in its entirety, this letter from the "Vicar of Christ:" "Very noble and well-beloved son, health and apostolic benediction. Having understood from several, and more especially from our beloved son Charles, Cardinal D'Armagnac, with what divine and very great affection thou dost defend the Catholic religion, and with what care and diligence thou dost strive to repress the vices of heretics, and to restore to its first state the observation of the Christian faith — works of a most true Christian and Catholic, and, without doubt, excellent gifts conferred by Heaven — we cannot and we ought not to neglect to return thanks to God who has on thee conferred so clear and sovereign an understanding, and rejoice with all our heart at thy great piety. More especially congratulating thee because that after having so happily fought under many virtuous kings and princes, and in so divers countries, thou art now called to maintain, with still greater glory, honour, and reputation, the war of the King of kings, Jesus Christ, and fight the fight of the Lord of Hosts. For this thou mayest assure thyself that His eternal favour will never fail thee, seeing that so gloriously and triumphantly thou defendest His good cause. We know well that thou hast no need of our exhortation to persevere in and pursue what thou hast so happily begun, but that thou hast laid the foundation of thy virtue on the holy and ardent affection that thou hast for the honour and glory of God. And our persuasion cannot more excite thee to virtuous and honourable deeds than the deeds themselves, so excellent and illustrious, recently done by thee in imitation of our most illustrious and beloved son, the King of Navarre (Anthony of Bourbon, the father of Henry IV), and many other sovereigns and illustrious lords of France. And this is what we now signify to thee in order that if before we have much loved, esteemed, and praised you for your excellent and magnanimous courage, your Christian good-will and holy affection to God, we may further incite thee thereto; and we declare that for this cause thou shalt find us, with the aid of God, ready to do all things that shall be in our power.

"Given at Rome at St. Peter's, under the ring of the Holy Fisherman. Of our Pontifical year the 3rd."

Take another story which points out clearly the "parting of the ways" in principle and practice between the two religions. In the days of Coligny a party of Huguenots, followers of his, crossed the ocean to Florida, and founded a little colony, where they might worship God in peace. They lived quietly and happily, tilling the soil and keeping on the best of terms with the neighbouring Indians. France and Spain were at peace at the time. Nevertheless, a Spanish fleet bore down upon the little settlement. A party of Spaniards landed, seized the unprepared and peaceful settlers, flayed them alive, and hung their bodies upon trees, placing over them the inscription, "Not as Frenchmen, but as 'heretics'." Of this breach of the law of nations the Court of France took no notice. "Heretics" were outlaws; in the eye of the law they had no existence. Those who had killed "also took possession" of the place, and built two forts for protection from the Indians, whom *they* had good cause to dread. But a Huguenot adventurer, named Dominique de Gourges, who heard of these things, secretly equipped a vessel in Rochelle, stole across the Atlantic, surprised the miscreants, and with the help of the Indians, slew, and afterwards hanged, every one of them. *He did not torture them*, but he hanged their bodies on the trees where they had hanged the Huguenots, reversing the inscription, which bore now, "Not as Spaniards, but as murderers." "Not as *Roman Catholics*, but as murderers" would have been more appropriate. And it throws what may be truly called a search-light upon the historical question between us and Rome.

It is very important that our ignorance on this subject should be dispelled, for it has done and is doing our cause much harm. When two people discuss a matter together, if one has no knowledge of the facts, and the other no regard for the truth, we know what results. There is a great conspiracy — we can call it no less — on the part of the Romanists and the Romanisers, to mislead us about the facts and the teachings

176

of history. If we are not well informed and well upon our guard, we shall fall into the traps that have been laid for us. The Jesuits have been particularly busy and skilful in this work. They have turned the Massacre of St. Bartholomew into "a mere squabble between the two parties, of which the Protestants happened to get the worst." Friends and foes knew better at the time. England knew better — and England's Queen, when after hearing the terrible story she received the Ambassador of France in deep mourning, with all her courtiers, dressed in mourning also, lining each side of the way he had to pass in solemn silence — no man giving him a word or a look of greeting. Lord Burghley knew better when he called the massacre "the most horrible crime that had been committed since the crucifixion of Christ," and Sir Thomas Smith, when he asked, *Will God sleep?*" The Emperor of Germany, the father-in-law of Charles IX, knew better when he wrote: "It is with great sorrow of heart I am informed that my son-in-law has suffered himself to consent to so foul a massacre. Gregory XIII knew better also, when in his joy he had the famous medal struck in commemoration of the event, and sent the golden rose, the special mark of his favour, to King Charles. We seem still to hear the thunder of the cannon of St. Angelo, the joyous peal from the bells of every steeple in Rome. And one sound yet more ominous lingers on the ear — the sound of a single solitary laugh. On hearing the tidings, Philip of Spain laughed aloud in his joy — the only time, it is said, when he was ever heard to laugh.

Not the St. Bartholomew Massacre alone, but the Revocation of the Edict of Nantes with its consequences takes on a different colouring in Jesuit and in all other history. In a recent History of France, compiled by Jesuits, all the horrors and cruelties that accompanied and followed that great crime are dismissed in a few airy words, and with the statement that "about fifty thousand persons withdrew from France, and were not ashamed to carry their knowledge, their strength, and their courage into the service of the stranger." Not a word of the horrible dragonnades, of the breakings on the wheel, of the dungeons, of the galleys — "those floating hells" — of the miseries of the children torn from their parents and the parents from their children! There are silences that lie more impudently than the loudest of uttered falsehoods. And thinking of this silence, I can only repeat what Pascal said two hundred and fifty years ago to one of these same Jesuits, *"Mentiris Impudentissime"* — "Thou dost lie most impudently."

The mention of Pascal reminds us of another result of our ignorance — a too great readiness to admire and copy certain Romish saints. Pascal lived and died in the Church of Rome, although he was enlightened enough to say, when his work against the Jesuits, *The Provincial Letters*, was condemned in Rome, "If my letters are condemned in Rome, what I condemn there is condemned in heaven." But, whatever his creed, *we love him!* Vinet, the Protestant theologian, asks, "Who is there that does not love Pascal?" Certainly not you or I! Thank God, we can look to meet him, and thousands who, like him, never left the Romish Church, in "the general assembly and church of the first-born, whose names are written in heaven." We have this great advantage over our opponents, that we are not obliged to think of them as they are of us, as inevitably lost and cast away. Practically, we are sure very many of them do *not* really think this — but it is what their Church declares. Thank God, *we* hold a larger, as well as a purer, faith. Joyfully, lovingly, we can recognize "the likeness of the Lord on every chastened face," whether it be the face of one whom Rome has burned or of one whom Rome has canonized.

Some of these last have been little worthy of our reverence — more worthy indeed of our execration, like St. Dominic, the founder of the Inquisition. But many, on the other hand, were true Christian men and women, who shone as lights —

though lights oftentimes dim and clouded — in the world of their own generation. And yet I cannot help deprecating the tendency shown by some of our friends to admire and to extol them, to study their lives and find therein inspirations and examples for their own, to the neglect of the great cloud of witnesses, the magnificent roll of saints, heroes, and martyrs that belong to us as Protestants. No doubt St. Francis of Assissi, St. Bernard, St. Teresa, St. Catherine of Siena, and others we could name, truly loved their Lord and ours — there is that great bond between us — and for that we can love them truly. But we are in no want of heroes and heroines, that we should go so far to seek them. If we will but study our Protestant history, we shall find abundant use for all the hero-worship we have got to spare. I would rather canonize St. Hugh Latimer, St. John Frith, St. William Tyndale, St. John Huss, and others I could mention — not to speak of a great company of more modern witnesses — than any of those whom Rome has sainted. Granted that to some of these God had manifestly given *the spirit of power and of love*, yet can we not add much more certainly with regard to our saints and heroes, *and of a sound mind*? It is a true remark however that Rome has canonized some whom under slightly altered circumstances she might have burned, and burned some who, had they been less clear-headed, courageous, and outspoken, she might have canonized. God grant us to enjoy, with all who have truly loved Him, the "sweet peace" of the heavenly home, when doubtless we shall get to know them, as they also will get to know us, in the presence of our common Lord.

We pass on to another hindrance, and a very grievous one, "the dangers caused by our unhappy divisions." These are a reproach continually brought against us by our foes — yes, and often by our friends; often too by ourselves, both in secret and in public, when — as indeed we ought to do — we pray to be delivered from them. And yet they are not all our fault, not even all perhaps entirely our misfortune.

Many of them were not, in the beginning, so much theological as historical and local. It was not because, when we came out from Rome, we were separated in faith that we were obliged at the time to form separate organizations. Groups of men came out at different times, in different places, and in different ways. They came out because they believed that the doctrines and the ceremonies of Rome were anti-scriptural; or, as it sometimes happened, Rome knew them before they knew themselves, and cast them out, when she could not kill them. Then they had to do, in each place, what St. Paul and the other Apostles did in primitive times — set things in order, have pastors ordained, provide for the administration of the Sacraments which Christ commanded, and so forth. At the time of the Reformation, it was only in some countries that they were able to do this. In others, as in Spain and Italy, they were exterminated, or driven into exile. But wherever they were able to hold their ground, they were obliged to organize. They could not help it; it was a necessity of their position. But you will ask, Why did they not unite and form one great, strong, Reformed Church all over Europe? That, even if they had wished it, would have been at the time simply impossible. You must not think that things in the sixteenth century were just as they are now; or that the reformer in Italy, who wished to take counsel with the reformer in England, had nothing to do but take a through ticket to London, put his foot in the train, and get there. He would have run a good chance of arriving instead in the kingdom of heaven, by the conveyance of a chariot of fire. It is true that, at intervals, some Protestants from some countries did manage to meet and confer together, but not frequently, and not generally.

So it was that every reformed community had to organize its own visible Church after its own ideas, and therefore came to be regarded as something apart and isolated. Suppose you see a field all covered with snow; by and by, when the sun rises and the snow melts in patches, every patch makes a little island of green amidst the white, and the field looks like a field of white, broken with isolated patches of green. But it is really the green which is one, underneath the snow, and this will appear presently, when the snow has all melted. At the time of the Reformation there was a real oneness underlying all the divisions of the reformed, and that in itself is a wonderful proof of the reality and the Divine origin of the great movement. When you think of it, does it not seem very remarkable that in the sixteenth century a number of men, quite apart from each other, in different countries and speaking different languages, just took the Bible in their hands, and, guided by God's Holy Spirit, drew from it the same conclusions? They rejected the same doctrines as inventions of men; they retained the same doctrines as truly revealed in Scripture; so that when they came to compare their several creeds and confessions they found them in wonderful harmony. What differences existed were almost entirely upon two subjects — the nature of the Sacraments, and the forms of Church government. These slight differences only serve to emphasize their universal agreement in all the main points of their belief. That all these men, working independently, found substantially the same things in the Bible is surely a striking proof that the things they found are those the Bible does really teach, and that the things they did not find are those the Bible does not teach.

Still, the divisions with which Protestants are so often reproached are not wholly historical and local. In all communities where people think, and where thought is free, some divisions are sure to arise. You cannot have perfect freedom and absolute unanimity together; the two things are incompatible. Differences are the outcome of the necessary limitations of our nature, and therefore are inevitable and invincible. No one of us sees things exactly as they are, and no one of us sees the whole of them. Each sees his own part, and sees it in his own way. Men are influenced in their opinions by temperament, by prejudice, by habit, by environment, by a hundred things; and when they are all free, there is nothing to hinder their proclaiming their differences openly. Indeed, they often talk more of a few small things about which they differ then of many great things in which they agree.

It would not be fair to look for the same freedom in the Church of Rome; it is an absolute monarchy, ruled by a head who is believed to be infallible. Yet Romanists cannot help having differences amongst themselves — the mind of modern Europe, even when fettered, is far too active for that — and their differences are often quite as keenly contested, and cause quite as much ill-will, if not more, than ours; only they are hidden from the eyes of the world by the screen of a so-called infallible authority, to which all profess to submit, though all do not do it very thoroughly.

Freedom develops party spirit. When Czar Alexander I was in England he studied our institutions with much interest. One day he said to Lord Castlereagh: "There is one of your English institutions which I greatly admire, and think very useful. I should like to introduce it into my country, but I do not know how."

"What is it, your Imperial Majesty?"

"Your Opposition," was the answer. He had watched the doings of our Parliament, and he thought the Opposition an admirable institution!

"Let your Majesty give your people a free Parliament, and they will give you an Opposition soon enough," was the answer.

In free communities there will be divisions, and there will be parties. These usually hinge, really or nominally, upon two principles or forces, each useful and necessary in its place. We find them in the stars of heaven as well as in the nations of the earth. By their action and reaction they control and balance each other, and the world goes on.

There are in every community some people whose main desire is to stand firm, and keep all the good they have — these may be said to represent the forces of Conservatism and Permanence. There are others who are always wanting to go on, and get all the good they can — these supply what may be called the forces of Advance and of Progress. Between these two, which modify or balance each other, the affairs of the world are managed — not very perfectly, as we can all of us bear witness, but still tolerably, and progress is made on the whole.

These two tendencies have always existed in Protestant as in other communities. On the Continent both are represented, though roughly and inexactly — the preservative tendency by the Lutheran Churches, the progressive by the Reformed. Indeed, in various ways and forms they show themselves everywhere. Nor, however troublesome, are such differences always or altogether to be deplored; because, as we have seen, the real and vital unity which subsists within and beneath them is a most striking proof of the truth of those principles which we hold in common. Let us cultivate this unity more and more. There are two places in which we can find and keep it — in the lofty place of personal communion with God, and in Him with each other; and in the lowly yet most honourable place of loving service to Him and to each other. In that loving service the only strife should be as to which of us shall do the most for our Master and our brethren.

Still, divisions are provoking — often very provoking indeed. We all know that. But, if we must needs be provoking and provoked, let us remember that there are two kinds of provocation. There is provoking "unto anger," and there is provoking "unto love and to good works." Let us choose the latter. And oh! What a glorious vision it opens out before us — the vision of a strong, pure, free, united Protestantism, standing with one front to the foe and with one heart for Christ, and against all that dishonours or denies Him! When that vision breaks on the sight, it seems almost too good to believe in — but it is not too good to hope for, to pray for, to strive for.

Another hindrance to our witness must not be ignored. It is a very great, but, as human nature is constituted, a quite unavoidable one. When the children of Israel left the land of Egypt, we are told that "a mixed multitude went up also with them." Probably never, before or since, has any nation or community gone up out of the house of bondage that a mixed multitude has not gone up with it. It was so at the time of the Reformation. When the great movement became, as in most countries it was forced to do, a political as well as a religious one, it was necessarily joined by this "mixed multitude," whose hearts were set on anything and everything but the restoration of a pure and spiritual religion. Some wanted civil liberty, others restrained license; many wanted relief from cruel oppression which they had long endured at the hands of both their spiritual and their temporal lords and masters; many more, maddened by their sufferings, burned for revenge upon their tyrants. Moreover, there were political schemers, who cared nothing at all about creeds or dogmas, but being, as we should call them now, opportunists, played upon the passions of the multitude in order to compass their own selfish ends. Just as the calamities that overtook the children of Israel in the wilderness were due in great measure to the mixed multitude, who murmured, disobeyed, and rebelled, so the sins and mistakes which have brought discredit upon our witness and disgrace upon our name are mainly due to our mixed multitude, who are or who have been with us, but not of us. "It must be that offenses come;" they are the fruit of human frailty and sin. But let us try to lessen their number by every effort in our power.

We come now to the last, and the worst, of all our hindrances. Shall we call it our Indifference? But what is indifference? Ruskin, that great teacher of Art — and of some other things too — tells us that vulgarity is "one of the many forms of death." The same thing may be said of indifference, and with even more truth, since it not only, like vulgarity, comes from "deadness of sensation," but it actually *is* deadness of sensation — in itself a beginning of death. And death is the one great thing we have to fight against — *the enemy*. Its sign and symptom is the absence of all feeling — all care. *Do* we feel? *Do* we care? Is it a matter of indifference to us what Faith we hold and accept, or what Faith the men and women of our country hold and accept, or in what Faith the children of our country are being brought up, and whether they are taught from their earliest years to read and love the Book which should be the guide of their youth, the inspiration of their manhood, and the stay and prop of their age? God keep the Bible for the men and the women and the children of our country! But God works by human hands. It is *we* who must do this work for Him, and it is as Protestants we must do it. First, some of us will say, we should do it for our own souls' sake, secondly for theirs. Yet after all there is a higher plea, a stronger motive, than even these — *"for Christ's sake."* Let us think of Christ; let love to Him and loyalty to Him be the strength which arms us for this great fight. But this presupposes *life in Christ*.

As a living Protestantism is the strongest thing in the world, so a dead Protestantism is the weakest. It is far weaker than a dead Romanism. For dead Romanism can make a great show before the world, can keep multitudes true to her claims, can even attract more multitudes to her standard, without any spiritual life at all. She knows how to dress out the corpse with beautiful raiment, and to lavish costly gems and flowers upon it. She knows how to give to the dead the spices of sweet and tender sentiment, the purple and fine linen of Art, the charms of music, and the glories of architecture. Some there are, indeed, who tell us that these gifts are not the best of their kind — that even in those things upon which she prides herself, Rome has failed. They tell us that her gold is tinsel, her ornaments tawdry and meretricious, and even her music but second-rate after all. But were it — as we know it has often been — like the music of the spheres, and her beauty "perfect" like that of Tyre, when she was "in Eden the garden of the Lord, and every precious stone was her covering, the sardius, the topaz, and the diamond" — we do not want a corpse, however beautiful and however splendidly adorned. There is no help in a dead thing; and least of all — again we must say it — is there help in a dead Protestantism.

For death there is but one remedy, and that is Life. When once death has come and life has gone, Nature knows nothing of its return: Life never comes back again to the House it has deserted. But above Nature there is a Power *that* can give life. There is ONE who has said that, "in the time that now is, the dead shall hear the voice of the Son of Man, and they that hear shall live." That word is true, as thousands amongst ourselves have proved and are proving every day. The life that Christ gives is a real life — no mere symbol or figure of speech, but a fact. It was this life which made the men and women of whom we have been telling, and who were often weak enough in themselves, strong to do and suffer all things, and able to rejoice with exceeding joy in the midst of anguish and in the face of death. It is this life of Christ — which is also the love of Christ — that we must have in our hearts; and this, and this alone, will make us victorious in our fight for Protestantism, which is, as we believe, the fight for truth, for freedom, and for righteousness.

The Reformation Trail Series

A collection of independent historical novels by mainly 19th century authors

(to be re-published D.V. in the first decade of the 21st Century)

Hubert Ellerdale by W. Oak Rhind
A tale of the days of Wycliffe

Crushed Yet Conquering by Deborah Alcock
A story of Constance and Bohemia
in the days of John Huss

Under Calvin's Spell by Deborah Alcock
A tale of the Heroic Times in Old Geneva

Prisoners of Hope by Deborah Alcock
A story of Faith in 16th century Bohemia

No Cross No Crown by Deborah Alcock
A tale of the Scottish Reformation

The Spanish Brothers by Deborah Alcock
A tale of the Sixteenth Century

Doctor Adrian by Deborah Alcock
A story of Old Holland

The King's Service by Deborah Alcock
A story of the Thirty Years' War

The William & Mary Trilogy
by Marjorie Bowen

The life of William III, Prince of Orange, Stadtholder of the United Netherlands, and King of England (with Queen Mary II) is one of the most fascinating in all of history. Both the author and the publisher of this book have been interested in this subject for many years. Although the story as told in this book is partly fictional, all the main events are faithful to history.

F. Pronk wrote in *The Messenger* about Volume 1: The author is well-known for her well-researched fiction based on the lives of famous historical characters. The religious convictions of the main characters are portrayed with authenticity and integrity. This book is sure to enrich one's understanding of Protestant Holland and will hold the reader spell-bound.

D.J. Engelsma wrote in *The Standard Bearer* about Volume 1: This is great reading for all ages, high school and older. *I Will Maintain* is well written historical fiction with a solid, significant, moving historical base . . . No small part of the appeal and worth of the book is the lively account of the important history of one of the world's greatest nations, the Dutch. This history was bound up with the Reformed faith and had implications for the exercise of Protestantism throughout Europe. Christian high schools could profitably assign the book, indeed, the whole trilogy, for history or literature classes.

C. Farenhorst wrote in *Christian Renewal* about Volume 1: An excellent tool for assimilating historical knowledge without being pained in the process, *I Will Maintain* is a very good read. Take it along on your holidays. Its sequel *Defender of the Faith*, is much looked forward to.

Time: 1670 - 1702   **Age: 14-99**

Volume 1 - *I Will Maintain*
  ISBN 0-921100-42-6   **Can.$17.95 U.S.$15.90**
Volume 2 - *Defender of the Faith*
  ISBN 0-921100-43-4   **Can.$15.95 U.S.$13.90**
Volume 3 - *For God and the King*
  ISBN 0-921100-44-2   **Can.$17.95 U.S.$15.90**

Israel's Hope and Expectation
by Rudolf Van Reest

G. Nederveen in *Clarion*: This is one of the best novels I have read of late. I found it captivating and hard to put down. Here is a book that is not time-bound and therefore it will never be outdated.

The story takes place around the time of Jesus' birth. It is written by someone who has done his research about the times between the Old and New Testament period. The author informs you in an easy style about the period of the Maccabees. . . Van Reest is a good storyteller. His love for the Bible and biblical times is evident from the start. He shows a good knowledge of the customs and mannerisms in Israel. Many fine details add to the quality of the book. You will be enriched in your understanding of the ways in the Old Testament.

Time: Inter-Testament Period   **Age: 15-99**
ISBN 0-921100-22-1   **Can.$19.95 U.S.$17.90**

For The Temple: A Tale of the Fall of Jerusalem
by G.A. Henty

Mr. Henty here weaves into the record of Josephus an admirable and attractive story. The troubles in the district of Tiberias, the march of the legions, the sieges of Jotapata, of Gamala, and of Jerusalem, form the impressive and carefully studied historic setting to the figure of the lad who passes from the vineyard to the service of Josephus, becomes the leader of a guerrilla band of patriots, fights bravely for the Temple, and after a brief term of slavery at Alexandria, returns to his Galilean home with the favour of Titus.

Time: 70 A.D.   **Age: 14-99**
ISBN 1-887159-00-2   **Can.$27.55 U.S.$18.99**

Against the World - The Odyssey of Athanasius
by Henry W. Coray

Muriel R. Lippencott in *The Christian Observer*: [it] . . . is a partially fictionalized profile of the life of Athanasius . . . who died in 373 AD. Much of the historical content is from the writing of reliable historians. Some parts of the book, while the product of the author's imagination, set forth accurately the spirit and the temper of the times, including the proceedings and vigorous debates that took place in Alexandria and Nicea. . . This is the story that Rev. Coray so brilliantly tells.

Time: 331 - 373 A.D.   **Age: 16-99**
ISBN 0-921100-35-3   **Can.$8.95 U.S.$7.90**

William of Orange - The Silent Prince
by W.G. Van de Hulst

Whether you are old or young you will enjoy this biography on the life of William of Orange. Read it and give it as a birthday present to your children or grandchildren. A fascinating true story about one of the greatest princes who ever lived and already by his contemporaries justly compared to King David.

Time: 1533 - 1584   Age: 7-99
ISBN 0-921100-15-9   Can.$8.95 U.S.$7.90

Three Men Came To Heidelberg and *Glorious Heretic*
by Thea B. Van Halsema

From the sixteenth-century Protestant Reformation came two outstanding statements of Faith: The Heidelberg Catechism (1563) and the Belgic Confession (1561). The stories behind these two historic documents are found in this small book. Frederick, a German prince, asked a preacher and a professor to meet at Heidelberg to write a statement of faith . . . The writer of the Belgic Confession was a hunted man most of his life. Originally he wrote the confession as an appeal to the King of Spain . . .

Time: 1560 - 1563   Age: 12-99
Cat. Nr. IP 1610   Can.$7.95 U.S.$5.95

Salt in His Blood — *The Life of Michael De Ruyter*
by William R. Rang

The greatest Dutch Admiral is an example of Christian love and piety, and fascinating because of his many true adventures as a sailer-boy, captain, and pirate-hunter.

Time: 1607 - 1676   Age: 10-99
ISBN 0-921100-59-0   Can.$10.95 U.S.$9.90

Struggle for Freedom Series
by Piet Prins

David Engelsma in the *Standard Bearer*: This is reading for Reformed children, young people, and (if I am any indication) their parents. It is the story of 12-year-old Martin Meulenberg and his family during the Roman Catholic persecution of the Reformed Christians in the Netherlands about the year 1600. A peddlar, secretly distributing Reformed books from village to village, drops a

copy of Guido de Brès' *True Christian Confession* — a booklet forbidden by the Roman Catholic authorities. An evil neighbor sees the book and informs . . .

Time: 1568 - 1572   Age: 10-99
Vol. 1 - *When The Morning Came* ISBN 0-921100-12-4   Can.$9.95 U.S.$8.90
Vol. 2 - *Dispelling the Tyranny*   ISBN 0-921100-40-X   Can.$9.95 U.S.$8.90
Vol. 3 & 4 are still to be translated and published.